I0504786

Lost Cosmos

Film Reviews That Never Made It To Cosmoetica.com

by

Dan Schneider

CONTENTS

Film Review Of *Ace In The Hole*
Copyright © by Dan Schneider, 2012

   Some films get worse in recall, as they have time to fester, and all of their flaws stick out, in memory, far more than their positive qualities. Such is the case with Billy Wilder's black and white 1951 film, *Ace In the Hole* (aka *The Big Carnival*), starring Kirk Douglas as a gung ho and fairly trite big city reporter, named Charles 'Chuck' Tatum, relegated to the sticks of Albuquerque, New Mexico, who stumbles upon a trapped fortune hunter, in a cave collapse, that he hopes will be a story the nation will eat up and catapult him back to national reportage prominence.
   The 111 minute film is well acted, solidly shot, and well coordinated, but utterly trite. There is not a single moment in the film that I did not see coming at least 20 minutes ahead of Time. Tatum is bound to find a BIG STORY, he's bound to meet an attractive woman- the trapped man's disgruntled wife- Lorraine Minosa (Jan Sterling), is bound to have sex with her, is bound to blackmail the big city papers into rehiring, is bound to lose it, and the trapped man- Leo Minosa (Richard Benedict), is bound to die because of Tatum's sleazy machinations. Finally, because it's a Billy Wilder film, there is bound to be a moralistic ending, and this really kyboshes the film, for Kirk Douglas simply is not a subtle actor, and moralism needs to be imparted with subtlety, lest it devolve into banal didacticism.
   In a rare confluence of deservedly subpar art meeting good criticism, this film became Wilder's first critical, as well as commercial, flop. Its acidic commentary on the media, while prescient, in the main, in its specifics it relies too much on stereotypes- of newspapermen, of podunk sheriffs- like Sheriff Kretzer (Richard Teal), of local rubery, of declassé wannabe femmes fatale, and so on. Some critics have labeled this a film noir, but it's really nothing of the sort. Yes, Tatum is a sleaze, and so is the local sheriff, but there are no crimes committed, and there is no female that sets the doom of the main character in motion, and, yes, Tatum seemingly dies at film's end, as well, his body falling straight at the camera, as he returns to the Albuquerque newspaper he had just quit, after a year's employment, to try and assuage the guilt he feels over killing the trapped man, by convincing the sheriff and contractor to take their time in rescuing him- which results in the man's death. But, Tatum, after possibly forcing himself on the trapped man's wife, then tries to strangle her with a cheap fur the trapped man bought her for a 5th wedding anniversary. She then stabs him in the side with a pair of scissors, and he lets it go untreated, then seemingly dies from the septic shock, after railing against the 'carnival' he incited.
   The screenplay, by Wilder, Walter Newman, and Lesser Samuels, is not a particularly good one, and the film score, by Hugo Friedhofer, veers into melodrama. The cinematography, by Charles B. Lang Jr. , is probably the best that the film has to offer, but even that is just serviceable. The break between Wilder and his long time screenwriting partner, Charles Brackett, shows. The film screened in a 1.33:1 aspect ratio, and the transfer is superb. Criterion did an excellent job of restoring the film, and even while streaming it on Netflix there is no noticeable damage.
   It's not that *Ace In The Hole* is a bad film, just a mediocre one, but one that could have easily been made better had a second pair of eyes been honed in on the screenplay, for almost all the film's flaws start with this area. That stated, the direction of Wilder, into the more obvious grotesques of each character, was also ham-handed. The film was based on two real life events: the Floyd Collins cave-in, in 1925, when he was trapped inside Sand Cave, Kentucky, which inspired reporter William Burke Miller, of the Louisville Courier-Journal, to write the tale of the doomed miner. Miller aced a Pulitzer Prize for his

trouble. The second event was the 1949 abandoned well death of Kathy Fiscus, in 1949. which was broadcast on the radio to a waiting nation. Both 'human interest stories' attracted thousands of gawkers to their scenes- although, unlike in the film, none had amusement rides nor a carnival spring up overnight, and the Fiscus death also was dramatized in Woody Allen's 1987 film, _Radio Days_.

  Ace In The Hole is a film that is in no way, shape, nor form, realistic, and its satire borders on comic, even though the film is also not a 'black comedy,' as some have labeled it. What it, and the screenplay, needed is some simple leavening by the injection of realistic characters into it, to lift it above the mere melodrama it is. Also, the final speech that Tatum gives, on top of the cliff face, railing about the death of Minosa, is simply too over the top, predictable, and corny. Yes, Douglas- an actor who could foment indignation with the best of them (see Stanley Kubrick's _Paths Of Glory_ if you doubt me), delivers the warmed over morality brilliantly, but, at film's end, it's still warmed over morality. Sans any realism, one is left with an entertaining, if empty, little treat, for even Kirk Douglas's charisma can only carry a film so far.

Film Review Of *The Seven Year Itch*
Copyright © by Dan Schneider, 2013

Marilyn Monroe was likely the least talented actress of all time to somehow become immortal. The astonishing thing is that, not only was she utterly void in acting, singing, and dancing skills, but even amongst the starlets of the 1950s- from Audrey Hepburn to Grace Kelly to Jayne Mansfield, she simply was not that good looking. In my review of Billy Wilder's vastly overrated 1959 comedy, *Some Like It Hot*, I detailed some of these flaws, but having just watched her earlier collaboration with Wilder, 1955's *The Seven Year Itch*, I can only shake my head in awe of how bad an actress she was.

Forget that the film was a toned down bowdlerization of George Axelrod's naughty Broadway comedy hit (by Axelrod himself) of the same name, and forget that the film even breaks down the fourth wall, to allow the main character, Richard Sherman (Tom Ewell), to muse that The Girl- the upstairs neighbor played by Monroe, might actually be 'Marilyn Monroe,' and even forget the famous post-date scene wherein Monroe, in a white dress, allows the breeze of a passing subway train blow up a grate and bare her legs for the audience to see. The fact of the matter is that there are some scenes in the film where, literally, one can see Monroe reading the cue cards- and not just in the Dazzledent tv commercials, where her character is 'supposed' to be so bad she needs to read cue cards. No, I mean in the actual diegetic tale within the film, and without the commercial. Yes, Monroe's four years of age younger difference, in this film, does allow her to be a bit more physically attractive than she was in *Some Like It Hot*, wherein her cottage cheesy look is galling, to say the least, for a sex symbol, but those four years of difference did, at least, allow Monroe to improve enough as an actress so that the audience could not actually see her reading her lines. So, it's a tradeoff, of sorts. But, on the whole, whereas the later film is a solid little comedy, overrated into a masterpiece, *The Seven Year Itch* is a yawnfest, and almost laughter free zone of film, with a few mild teehees that randomly bubble to the surface.

The film opens with a pointless gag about American Indians on Manhattan, in the 1400s, sending off their squaws for the summer, as they chase single women, then it follows Sherman- a Walter Mitty-like middle-aged publishing executive of pulp fiction books, through the first few days of a summer alone without his wife and son, who are sent to Maine for vacation. His wife Helen (Evelyn Keyes) and son Ricky (Butch Bernard) have unwittingly left the boy's kayak paddle behind, and the film follows Sherman's attempts to mail the thing to his wife, whom he suspects of cheating on him with a bad pulp writer named Tom MacKenzie (Sonny Tufts). To combat his loneliness and run amok imagination (he fantasizes of trysts with his secretary, a nurse, and his wife's best friend, aping the iconic beach scene in *From Here To Eternity*), he starts hanging out with The Girl, who has sublet the apartment above him from vacationing neighbors. This occurs after she almost kills him by knocking a flowerpot off of he balcony. She is a spokemodel on tv, and stirs up feelings in Sherman, to the point that he contacts the psychiatrist author of a sex book his company is publishing, Dr. Brubaker (Oskar Homolka), for whom the term *seven year itch* is derived. He also feels as if he might be living out the life of the lead character in Oscar Wilde's tale, *The Picture Of Dorian Grey*.

The rest of the film follows Sherman in his fantasies about The Girl, with her either knowingly or not bringing him to the Eisenhoverian equivalent of a mindgasm. When they play Chopsticks at his piano, he makes a pass at her, and they flop over on the piano bench and on to the floor. In actuality, this is the shot that gives the best view of Monroe's legs, not the subway breeze scene. Nonetheless, by today's standards, one still has to wonder what appeal Monroe had over men, especially in contrast to so many of the better looking and more talented starlets of her day.

The subway scene, incidentally, comes after the duo have gone out on a date, to see *The Creature From The Black Lagoon*, and throughout the bulk of the film, Sherman tries to hide his near-trysts from a nosy plumber, also summer single and on the make, called Crehoulis (Victor Moore). The film ends with MacKenzie coming to pick up the kayak paddle, only to have Sherman jealously knock him out with one punch, then determine to take two weeks of vacation, regardless of what his boss wants, and drive up to Maine, as The Girl implores him to do so, kisses him goodbye, and the film ends with him rushing to his care, forgetting his shoes, which are tossed out the window to him by The Girl.

And, in sum, that's it. That is the whole of this film, oft called a classic. It is, instead, probably the worst Billy Wilder film I've seen to date. Granted, the caveat is that it is still Billy Wilder, so it is only bad in comparison to the rest of his canon. Overall, it's a mediocre little film. Ewell does well with the limited role he is given, but the platitudes and attitudes he owns are horribly dated, and just plain silly. The rest of the cast ranges from barely passable to awful (Monroe). The screenplay is, aside from the casting of Monroe, the film's biggest bane- and Axelrod and Wilder's capitulation to the censors, sans any real clever ways to undermine such censorship, is an example of cowardice and stupidity. Milton Krasner had little to do in the way of cinematography, since the whole film was shot on a soundstage. Ditto can be said of the editing of Hugh S. Fowler and the scoring of Alfred Newman. This generic formula approach only makes the lack of a subversive script all the more glaring. Fortunately, the color film only runs 105 minutes, although, in reality, trimming a good 25-30 minutes would have helped the film move along, and avoid the repetitions of Sherman's repeated clumsiness in front of The Girl.

Oh, but what might have been, as numerous legends abound of an unbowdlerized script, and a possible pairing of Walter Matthau and Gena Rowlands in the lead roles. Then, perhaps, this might have been a minor masterpiece! Unfortunately, we are stuck with a bad script and the eternally talentless Norma Jeane Baker playing the only role she could play in life- Marilyn Monroe, and that's what has to be recognized for this film to even succeed at a minor level: Monroe was her own invention, and in all of her film roles- minor or major, she can only play who she was in real life. The Girl *IS* Marilyn Monroe for Marilyn Monroe was the only role Marilyn/Norma could play, and far from the claims of many critics that Monroe's 'character' was 'all innocence,' 'spontaneous,' or 'lacking in self-awareness,' the reality is that Monroe was HYPER-AWARE of her only created role, to the point that it utterly blinded her to not only any of the subtleties of acting, nor other performing arts, but her own narcissism and flaunting of her sexuality is so precisely calculated to render male critics, especially, incapable of seeing her MASSIVE flaws as a performer of any worth.

Regardless, without the original play, dated as it is anyway, the film was doomed to fail. Ewell, as mentioned, is the only positive in the film- sort of a pre-*Bewitched* Darren, but even that is but a barely registered positive. That this morass of mediocrity was let loose by Billy Wilder, one of the best screenwriters of the mid-20th Century, is even more disappointing. Nonetheless, *The Seven Year Itch* has a few moments of charm, and is, even in its failure, inoffensive. Would that so many other of the more recent mediocrities unleashed by Hollywood contain such qualities, then the filmgoing public would not be so eager to flock to other media. **Note to Hollywood hacks**: Watch Wilder, even when bad! Why? Because he's still better than you!

DVD Review of *Shadow Of A Doubt*
Copyright © by Dan Schneider, 2010

    Alfred Hitchcock's initial 'American' film, 1943's black and white, 108 minute long *Shadow Of A Doubt*, was reputedly Hitchcock's favorite film from his canon, and there's little doubt that it's a good, solid film, and a film that is in the top third of his canon, qualitatively. But, it simply is nowhere near a great film for many of the same reasons later, and more famous, films of his fail.

    The film is a fairly uncomplicated tale about a serial killer who visits his sister's family to escape a nationwide manhunt. Charles 'Charley' Oakley (Joseph Cotton) is hiding from detectives in a New Jersey slum, and makes his way past his tail, in scenes shot outdoors, that show a remarkable facility for exteriors by Joseph Valentine. It is quite jarring in that most Hitchcock films were shot on stages, while the gritty realism displayed shows a world of potential that Hitchcock would rarely exploit (even in *The Wrong Man*, a gritty film based upon a real life story, Hitchcock stuck to mostly sets). Yet, this sets the tome for the film; the bulk of which was shot on locations. He then takes a train cross-country, to head to his sister Emma Newton's (Patricia Collinge) home in Santa Rosa, California (where most of the film was shot). She is an aging housewife, whose husband Joseph (Henry Travers- Guardian Angel Clarence from *It's A Wonderful Life*) is a bank teller that engages in theoretical murderous plotting with his nerdy neighbor Herbie Hawkins (Hume Cronyn) for fun. The couple has three children, in ascending age, Roger (Charles Bates), Ann (Edna May Wonacott), and Charlotte 'Charley' (Teresa Wright), who was named for her uncle, whom she feels is her psychic twin. This is 'proven' to her when she goes to telegram him to come for a visit, only to receive his telegram that he is on a train to visit them.

    It seems Uncle Charley is an itinerant, who has traveled the world, and done well, financially. Why he is a suspect in crimes is not immediately known, Shortly after his arrival, two men show up claiming to be pollsters for a national survey. They are Jack Graham (Macdonald Carey) and Fred Saunders (Wallace Ford). The two are really detectives, and after Uncle Charley avoids them, Jack asks young Charley out for a date. There, he informs her, off camera, that her uncle may be the Merry Widow Murderer, a man wanted for the seduction and murder of three wealthy Eastern widows. Here, the film falls into melodrama, and the Dumbest Possible Action trope, because supposedly there is a second suspect in New England who is being tailed, but since this killer is known to have consorted with women in power, his identification would be rather easy, not like that of a Jack The Ripper-type killer who springs from the darkness and leaves a trail of corpses in his wake.

    At first young Charley refuses to believe such, but having caught her uncle hiding things, and giving her a ring with the initials of the last murdered woman and her husband. Later, at supper, her uncle (whom she earlier saw flirting, at her father's bank, with one of her town's wealthier widows) gives this speech:

> The cities are full of women; middle-aged widows, husbands dead, husbands who've spent their lives making fortunes, working and working. And then they die and leave their money to their wives, their silly wives. And what do the wives do, these useless women? You see them in the hotels, the best hotels, every day by the thousands, drinking the money, eating the money, losing the money at bridge, playing all day and all night, smelling of money, proud of their jewelry, but of nothing else. Horrible, faded, fat, greedy women.

And when his niece objects that they are still human beings, he retorts, '*Are they human or are they fat, wheezing animals, hmm? And what happens to animals when they get too fat and too old?*'

Uncle Charley is soon wise to his niece's suspicions and vows to leave, as long as she keeps quiet, so as to not 'upset' her mother, his sister, who idolizes him. Here now is another failure of the film, for it inhabits a Norman Rockwell America. It's 1943, and gangsterism and mass murder from the Second World War are in the headlines. It's simply not tenable to believe a decent and intelligent girl like Charley (who is college aged) would not turn her uncle in, just to protect her mother's feelings. Also, she has to be smart enough to know he will try to kill her. But then, the other suspect in the slayings ends up killed while fleeing capture, and it is assumed he did so because he was guilty. This removes the two detectives from Uncle Charley, but not before an absurd love story interjects, with Jack confessing his love for young Charley after a single date, and even hinting at marriage when he returns to town after another case.

So, Uncle Charley is in the clear, but reneges on his deal to leave. He stays, and antagonizes his niece, and twice tries to kill her, by tampering with a step on a stairway and locking her in a garage with a car motor running. Twice she survives, but she wears the ring from the dead woman to scare him off, after he gives a speech to a local women's club, makes a massive donation to the local hospital, and is regaled as a hero. The next day, after saying goodbye to his clan, Uncle Charley forces his niece to stay on the train, and then attempts to push her out a door. This is one of the silliest and most contrived endings in all Hitchcockdom. First, he should easily be able to force her out. Second, he, of course, ends up being pushed out by her. Third, a train is coming in the other direction, naturally. The film's coda takes place after a large funeral wherein Uncle Charley is regaled as a great man, as young Charley, and a returned Jack Graham muse on Charley's cynicism, and keeping her uncle's crimes a secret.

Technically, the film is solid, with a good waltz score by Dimitri Tiomkin, but the screenplay by playwright Thornton Wilder (of *Our Town* fame), Sally Benson, and Hitchcock's wife, Alma Neville, is merely passable. The film's limited success rides on the star acting performances of Wright, as the only character who experiences any growth in the film, and Cotton- cast against type, as one of Hitchcock's best murderers; although what turned him from a sweet young boy into a killer is never known. The closest answer comes when Emma recounts a childhood accident that almost killed Charley. Throughout the film the two Charleys are often shown in opposing positions physically- whether loafing on beds, or staring at each other across a table, and there is a hint of sexual tension between the two; at least what little the censors would allow in those days. In many of the film's twinnings, the relationship between the two Charleys also mirrors that between Emma and her brother, save that the mother figure has an unhealthy obsession with her sibling. Another is how young Charley initially feels her uncle's arrival will liven her life up while he seeks refuge to calm his down.

But, the film has too many plot holes, and a suspension of disbelief, in a film so aching for realism, is hard to come by when, as mentioned, the film is propelled by Dumbest Possible Action tropes, and ends so poorly. Far more effective would have been letting the real guilt or innocence of Uncle Charley remain in doubt. Yes, this was the Hays Code Era, and villains needed a comeuppance, but there would have been ways around that. The obvious would have been to leave his guilt, thereby his need for punition, in doubt. As example, after Uncle Charley is 'cleared' by the other suspect's death, young Charley could have wondered if the two close calls she had were accidents or not, with her uncle's presence in them kept from the viewers, and then have the film end with her noticing that her uncle is traveling with the rich widow they both met at her father's bank.

The DVD, from Universal, part of the Alfred Hitchcock *The Masterpiece Collection*, has a few nice bonus features: production photos, publicity stills, production drawings and a theatrical trailer. There is also a half hour long featurette on the film called *Beyond Doubt*. It has interviews with surviving actors, as well as behind the scenes trivia from Hitchcock's daughter Pat. And, for trivia buffs, the old man's cameo comes on the train to Santa Rosa, as he is seen playing cards with a doctor.

While *Shadow Of A Doubt* is a well made film, it is too much of a classic mid-Twentieth Century melodrama to be claimed as great- a flaw too many Hitchcock films suffer from. Plot dominates character, even though there is a good deal of good character dialogue amongst the minor characters, there is the ridiculous and gratuitous 'love story' angle, as well as Hitchcock's over-reliance on simplistic Freudian motivations, and the poor ending, compounded by the fact that it is done with very poor rear projection, all of which makes the film merely solid; far from the 'masterpiece' its inclusion in the Universal collection would indicate, and that its greatest proponents claim. Still, Wright and Cotton make it an enjoyable diversion for a couple of hours. There are worse things in this world; right Charley?

DVD Review Of *The Petrified Forest*
Copyright © by Dan Schneider, 2010

The 82 minute long, 1936 black and white film adaptation of Robert Sherwood's hit Broadway play, *The Petrified Forest*, is, today, most well known for signaling the arrival of Humphrey Bogart as an actor of force in Hollywood, rather than being an audacious cinematic polemic, which it was seen as in its day. But, the truth is that, despite the fact that Bogart went on to bigger and better things, it would be several years before his breakthrough to A list stardom after *High Sierra* and *The Maltese Falcon*. The next few years would see Bogart bounce between supporting roles in both A and B films, usually playing slimy gangsters, often shot to death by Jimmy Cagney.

The film, though, is not all Bogart. In fact, he does not make his presence in the film until 36 minutes in to it, in a 'star entrance' second to only Orson Welles' entrance as Harry Lime in *The Third Man*. By 'star entrance' I refer to when a character is mentioned over and again before their actual appearance. In this mode, Bogart's Duke Mantee is certainly the most powerful presence in the film, but he's not the star. In fact, in the film, Bogart is accorded only 5th billing, behind Leslie Howard (as Alan Squier)- then a huge star, Bette Davis (as Gabby Maple)- then a rising star, soon to win an Oscar for her work in *Dangerous*, Genevieve Tobin- who played a socialite- Mrs. Chisholm, and Dick Foran, who played Boze, a dopey jock.

The film opens with some scene setting in the Petrified Forest area of Arizona (really some rather cheesy sets), and a shot of British sojourner Alan Squier hitchhiking. He is a failed writer and a divorcee, after having spent many years sponging off of a rich woman. He happens upon a run down diner and gas station, called the Black Mesa Bar-B-Q, owned by Jason Maple (Porter Hall)- a World War One veteran who is on his way to a vigilante meeting set up to help capture Mantee and his gang; his artsy dreamer daughter, Gabby; and Gabby's grandfather (Charley Grapewin), an old codger type who bullshits about his youth in the old Wild West, even claiming to have been shot at (and missed) by Billy The Kid. Gabby is squarely in the romantic crosshairs of Boze, who quickly gets possessive of her when she and Alan hit it off, when she shows him her paintings and tells him of her dreams to go to France, where her mother lives, and who sends her books of poetry, including a Modern Library edition of the poems of Francois Villon. Boze chases Alan away, after he cannot pay for a meal, but Gabby give it to him gratis, then even gives him a dollar coin, as 'change,' after she arranges for him to get a ride to Phoenix with a rich couple, Mr. and Mrs. Chisholm (Paul Harbey and Tobin).

That's when Duke Mantee, 'world famous killer'- after a notorious massacre in Oklahoma City- and his gang enter. They stop the rich couple's car, and head back to the diner, where they take all hostage, including Alan and the rich couple and their chauffer, Joseph (John Alexander), who also return, when a sandstorm hits. A number of intrigues occur, as well as personal revelations, and after Boze foolishly tries to fight back, he is taken away and tied up by Gabby and one of Duke's men. This is when Alan makes a pact with Duke for Duke to kill him, so that Gabby can get the $5000 from his life insurance policy to travel to France. Duke agrees, but then the diner is besieged by the vigilantes. Duke and his men try to flee, but Alan stands in his way. Duke refuses to kill him for no real reason, until Alan leaves him no choice. The gangsters get away, but it is soon revealed that they have been killed by the vigilantes offscreen. The film ends with Gabby holding Alan's body and planning on burying him out in the petrified forest.

While the film was mostly shot on soundstages, journeyman director Archie Mayo and cinematographer Sol Polito do sneak in some deft camera angles and symbolism into some of their compositions, such as shots showing Duke beneath a rack of antlers that gives him a Satanic look, or the positioning of the two lone black characters, chauffer Joseph and Duke's henchman, Slim (Slim Thompson)- who seems to be an equal to Duke's two other white cronies, during a humorous exchange where Slim chides Joseph for his Stepin Fetchit like demeanor, only part of the film's political dynamic that pits the rich against the poor (this was the Great Depression), haves against have nots, artists against industrialists, and the little man individualist against the socialite conformist. Exchanges like that between the two black characters are highlights of a good screenplay by Delmer Daves and Charles Kenyon, adapted from Sherwood's play. Another good moment comes when Duke takes offense to Alan's belittling of Gramps Maple. It shows, along with his reluctance to kill Alan or the others without cause, and with his sense of politesse, that he is not a mere stereotype- despite some of the mannerisms Bogart affects in his portrayal, reputedly modeled after those of real life gangster John Dillinger. In fact, his portrayal of Mantee is one of the better performances Bogart ever gave onscreen, for it cuts against his later obnoxious 'Bogey' persona so well. Howard is actually quite good as the dewy eyed dreamer from the U.K. And Davis gives an affecting performance as Gabby. Even Tobin shines in the few scenes where she charts her life of doom as a society matron whose marriage was picked by her parents.

One wishes, in fact, that the film could have had another 15-20 minutes of running time to let some of the character interplay develop. Reputedly the film version, indeed, is significantly shorter than the stage version, in which Howard and Bogart were the stars, as well. The film also does a good job in its portrayal of the dynamic between those characters who are able to grow- like Gabby, and possibly Duke, and all the rest who have petrified into their assigned roles. This duplicity of meaning in the film's title is a subtlety lost on many critics, both at its release and now, but nonetheless adds a power to the film for those who can discern its relevance.

The Warner Brothers DVD is a good package. The film's visual quality is quite good, and the film is seen in a 1.33:1 aspect ratio. The DVD is part of a 6 disk Warner Brothers Gangsters Collection. The extra features are very good, for the DVD tries to present the film as it would have been shown in theaters, in a section called Warner Night At The Movies. Hosted by film critic Leonard Maltin, the segment features cartoons, newsreels, trailers and short subject films from the same year as the film in the DVD- this one being 1936. There are trailers, a musical short- *Rhythmitis*, and a cartoon, The Coo Coo Nut Grove. There is also a radio play of the film, starring Bogart, Tyrone Power, and Joan Bennett. The featurette on the film is good, called *The Petrified Forest: Menace In The Desert*. Assorted film experts reminisce on the film and its impact. There is also the original theatrical trailer for *The Petrified Forest*. The film commentary features film historian and Bogart biographer Eric Lax. It's a good, solid commentary, with info on the characters and their portrayers given as each first appears onscreen. It's not as deep nor learned as some of the best commentaries I've heard, but it's significantly better than the majority, even if there are a few spots where Lax takes a few minutes' respite from comment

The Petrified Forest is not a great film, and its discourse is a bit too didactic, compared to post-New Wave films that dealt with similar themes, in America and globally- such as the social dramas of the 1960s; but it is still a good film, and well above most of the films made in its day, or ours. It is simultaneously universal and timeless, yet also an artifact of its day- see the scene where the diner and Davis boast that they do not accept tips, as it is Un-American, so keep your change. Nowadays, tipping is seen as a right, not a gratuity. But, the film's power- and unfortunately continuing relevance- lies mainly in its seemingly naïve 'will to power.' It openly flaunts its contempt for American injustice, from an early scene where Jason Maple argues politics with a telephone line repairman to its many discourse on the exploitation of workers, rampant corporatism, the repression of women, blacks, the failure of artists, the rise of gangsterism, the American government's ineffectiveness, and the death of personal strength- these days symbolized by the sway of Political Correctness and Postmodernism. It is a film that is political, but never to the point that its politics subverts its art. This is when art truly can be potent politically- a point almost all so-called 'political artists' miss. *The Petrified Forest* does not miss it, and that's why it still has life when viewed today, for, unlike its protagonist, it is not a faded thing of the past, although, because of all the social flaws it attacks, it would be nice to see it made redundant, even if still an enjoyment to view.

DVD Review of *Rio Bravo*
Copyright © by Dan Schneider, 2010

  Howard Hawks' hour and twenty minute long 1959 color Western film, *Rio Bravo*, starring John Wayne, is usually bandied about with the usual suspects as among the best Westerns ever made. Among that list are Hawks' own *Red River*, John Ford's *The Searchers*, Sergio Leone's *Once Upon A Time In The West*, and Sam Peckinpah's *The Wild Bunch*. Among that list, though, only Leone's film can really be considered great cinema, beyond its genre, for only it ever portrays its characters as people in a certain psychological situation that happens to be set in the West, rather than people who are merely from the West. Ford's film is mere solid entertainment, as is Peckinpah's, and *Red River* is definitely deeper, better, and more visually western than *Rio Bravo*- much of which was shot in a studio. But the western that this film is most often linked to is Fred Zinneman's *High Noon*, starring Gary Cooper. This is because both Hawks, and *Rio Bravo* star John Wayne claimed they made their film as an answer to what they considered the unmanliness of *High Noon*, wherein Cooper's lead character, a sheriff, goes about town looking for help to fight off the bad guys. To Hawks and Wayne, both macho men, this was anathema. Of course, this is also what makes the Zinneman film more realistic and relevant to audiences today. *Rio Bravo*, by contrast, is merely a nice casual entertainment, and Wayne is at his macho best, with both his male compatriots, and female love interest, a young, leggy, and sexy Angie Dickinson.
  The film is decidedly lightweight, but has many light, comic moments, including some involving Wayne, who is actually likeable in his role. The tale is rather simple: in an unnamed small town in Presidio County, Texas, near the Rio Bravo (Rio Grande), a drunken deputy sheriff named Dude (Dean Martin), is groveling for a coin tossed into a spittoon by an outlaw named Joe Burdette (Claude Akins). His boss, Sheriff John T. Chance (Wayne) kicks the spittoon away. After some slugfests, Burdette heads to another bar, after shooting a man who tried to break up the fight. Chance follows Burdette, to arrest him, and Dude helps him overcome Burdette's goons. They take Burdette away to jail. Burdette's brother, Nathan (John Russell),then spends much of the rest of the film plotting to free his brother before the arrival of a U.S. Marshal in a few days. Naturally, much killing ensues. There end up being two other deputies, an old cripple named Stumpy (Walter Brennan), and a young gun named Colorado Ryan (Ricky Nelson, of *The Adventures Of Ozzie And Harriet* fame). They end up, of course, defeating the bad guys, and Wayne's Chance ends up successfully bedding and wooing the mysterious gambling gal known only as Feathers (Dickinson).
  The film has some moments of excellence, especially in terms of acting. Brennan is delightful as the ultimate Western sidekick deputy; Wayne is likeable in his best and most human performance; Dickinson is coy and sexy- and her love story with Wayne is too lightheartedly fun to be intrusive, and even Martin is solid as the drunk trying to turn his life around; although his best moments come when not being drunk. Martin tends to overact his 'drunk' scenes, while being pretty good in his sober ones. About the only mediocre performance is turned in by Nelson, who needs to resort to facial tics to try to imbue his character with depth, although he does admirably well in the physical scene where he saves Wayne from an ambush by three of the Burdette men. There are some down moments, such as when Nelson, Martin, and Brennan sing a few tunes, and the film is really more of a multiple character portrait than an exciting 'Western,' but the most telling thing about the film- from its blazing color cinematography to its witty banter- is how influenced by television westerns it is, especially when compared to the other westerns I mentioned. The antics of Brennan and some of the supporting Mexican

characters are also very tv-like, as well as stereotypical. The cinematography, by Russell Harlan, is the usual solid fare in a Hawks film- even considering how little western scenery is used, and the screenplay, by Jules Furthman and Leigh Brackett, based on a short story by B.H. McCampbell, has its ups and downs, as mentioned. The best work in the film comes from a classic western score by Dimitri Tiomkin.

The Warner Brothers DVD package is made of two disks. Disk one has the film, shown in a 1.85:1 aspect ratio. It also has a gallery of theatrical trailers of John Wayne films. There is also an audio commentary track that is shared by film director John Carpenter (whose films *Assault On Precinct 13* and *Ghosts Of Mars* were both inspired by *Rio Bravo*) and film critic Richard Schickel. Neither man gives any insights that are of any depth. Both convey mostly awe for the film, even in moments when it's rather pedestrian. Schickel, especially, is nihil in his contribution, but both men often say nothing for long periods of time. Disk two contains three featurettes. *Old Tucson: Where Legends Walked* is a short film about the studio built town that was built to film westerns, and where this film was shot. *Commemoration: Howard Hawks' Rio Bravo* is a half hour long piece that focuses on the film and its making. Then there is the excellent hour long documentary, created by Schickel, called *The Men Who Made The Movies; Howard Hawks*, which is a good profile of the director's life and career. It is narrated by filmmaker Sydney Pollack.

Rio Bravo is a good, solid film, and as many highly entertaining moments, but it simply comes nowhere near greatness. Put aside even comparing it with the then contemporaneous films coming out of Europe, which boldly dealt with sexuality and philosophy, from directors like Federico Fellini, Ingmar Bergman, Michelangelo Antonioni, or the great Japanese cinema being created by the likes of Yasujiro Ozu, Akira Kurosawa, Masaki Kobayashi, and Kenji Mizoguchi, and this film just does not compare with the psychological depth and stylized realism of *High Noon*, nor even Hawks' earlier *Red River*. In many ways it shares much more in common with its television siblings, *Gunsmoke* and *Bonanza*, save for being over twice as long as their episodes. Its biggest flaw, and one shared by most pop films, is that its narrative is propelled by the Dumbest Possible Action trope. Almost every major development in the film, that goes against Chance and his people, comes about through their own stupidity, sloth, or carelessness. That, and the fact that the film could have easily been improved by cutting its excesses down to 90 minutes, means that *Rio Bravo* is highly flawed, despite its enjoyability factor. Go in expecting a cinematic masterpiece, one of the greatest films of all time, and you will be left sorely wanting. Go in just looking for a good old film to make you smile after a hard day's work, and *Rio Bravo* is the ticket. Don't say I never done you no favors, now, pardnuh!

Film Review Of *Bernie*
Copyright © by Dan Schneider, 2013

Richard Linklater's 2011 comedy mockumentary *Bernie*, a 104 minute long film based upon a real life 1990s murder in the eastern Texas town of Carthage, is a good film, with the best performance of his career by Jack Black, as the titular murderer, Berne Tiede. Having stated that, it has to be added that that is all the film is- a good film, with a good performance by a lead actor known for his scenery chewing comedies and over the top schtick, it is not great, nor is Black's performance great acting. Oftentimes, comedians are way overpraised for acting performances that require a little more depth, and this is true of Black's performance. Similar overpraise has been lavished on comedian cum actors like Jamie Foxx, Jim Carrey, Jerry Lewis, and others.

The film mixes real documentary style interviews of local residents of Carthage, talking of the real Tiede, and the real murder, from 1996, while we see 'flashbacks' with the film's main characters portrayed by actors. It's a nice touch that blurs the boundaries of reality, and the fictive tale is moved up a decade or more, for we see Bernie and his lover/employer, the widow Marjorie Nugent (Shirley MacLaine) routinely conversing on cell phones that were not around in the 1990s.

The film opens with Tiede, as an assistant mortician who may or may not be a homosexual. He is well liked in the community, and supports the church, as well as directing local arts fairs and musicals. Nugent is the wealthiest woman in town, as well as the nastiest, and soon Tiede and her become 'companions.' Townsfolk debate whether or not they were lovers, but they definitely became companions, and Tiede leaves the funeral home to become her manager and personal assistant. Slowly, Nugent alienates Tiede from his friends and activities, and abuses and fires all her other employees. One day, not long after Nugent confining Tiede to the property, Tiede snaps (in the film- in real life, this is debatable), picks up a beebee gun, and shoots Nugent four times in the back. The old woman dies and Tiede stuffs her body in a garage freezer, presumably to later give her a proper burial.

After nine months of stalling and explaining away Mrs. Nugent's whereabouts, and giving away donations to various people and organizations in town, Tiede is caught and confesses. But, he is so well liked, and Nugent so despised, that local DA Danny Buck Davidson (Matthew McConaughey) asks for a change of venue. Usually it is because a defendant is so hated, not so well liked, that the state feels a fair trial is impossible. The trial is held in nearby San Augustine, and Davidson gets Tiede sentence to life imprisonment. The film then ends with outtakes of the townsfolk preening away with their opinions.

Overall, the performances are all good, solid- but nothing great, and the musical numbers, within the film, that Tiede directs, are the most amazing part of the film, considering that, in real life, high school and local musicals are uniformly bad. As a comedy, the film scores some points, but it's never laugh out load funny, the way a mockumentary like *This Is Spinal Tap* is. On the documentary side, the film has the feel of an Errol Morris film, albeit utterly lacking in the acidic look at human nature. The film is clearly pro-Tiede whereas it should have had a bit more ambiguity, to better highlight the comedy. Humor is often best when the basest aspects of human nature are explored.

As example, the DA suggests that Tiede deliberately alienated Nugent from her family, and the film does, indeed, show that Tiede took over Nugent's life as much as she did his, but it never goes with even broaching the idea that Tiede deliberately set up Nugent to murder her for her money, even though all his actions were straight out of a 1940s

Hollywood film noir of a gigolo. And, like it or not, that is what Tiede was, for the 'relationship' between the two, even if not sexual, was certainly ethically inappropriate.

The screenplay, co-written by Linklater and Skip Hollandsworth, a reporter who first wrote of the murder in a 19989 Texas Monthly article, is solid, but not spectacular. If not for the 'gimmick' of using real people as talking heads in a mockumentary, the film would not have had the little resonance it does, as the local Greek chorus grounds the film whenever the scenes start to get a little too outlandish to be believed. That said, sometimes the choral elements undercut certain scenes, or, some scenes are utterly registered as superfluous, as we are first told about them, in hilarious gossipy fashion, then see the scene play out in a rather blasé manner. The cinematography and scoring is solid, at best, so the deciding factor comes down to the performances, which are just good enough to sell the whole conceit. The film also makes good comic use of intertitle cards, in a nod to silent films.

In no way, shape, nor form is *Bernie* a great film, filled with great performances. It is just a small, sad, yet funny little film about a sad situation that could have easily been avoided, and just as easily been exploited by Linklater. It is not. Making any more of it, though, is pointless, even as making it was not.

Film Review Of *Humble Pie*
Copyright © by Dan Schneider, 2012

   The 2007 independent film comedy, *Humble Pie* (aka *American Fork*), is almost an archetypal film. By that I mean that if you were to try to imagine an 'independent film comedy,' you would likely envision a film quite like it. It is a film about a lovable loser who lives in a town that shuns him, works at a job with no future, has some wacky adventures with people of dubious character, and has a family situation that only exacerbates these trends. In the end, of course, all works out, in the sense that he learns a lesson, and his life ends up pretty much the same as it did at the film's start- in this case, taking a driver's test for a license that will make him feel like 'somebody.'

   Having stated that, the film, while predictable, is often very funny. There is no great acting, no great cinematography, no great depth....but it all works. The film follows fat grocery clerk Tracy Orbison (Hubbel Palmer), who works at an unspecified small town, in the American West, independent supermarket called *Legrands*. He writes doggerel in a marble notebook (his 'Book of Secrets') he always totes around, does not get along with his co-workers- such as Helen- a handicapped bitch (Rae Ritke), and dreams of being an actor, all the while trying to mentor a group of the small town's juvenile delinquents. His mother (Kathleen Quinlan) is a divorced shrew who hates him, because he looks like his father (she calls him 'her misguided son') and his sister, Peggy (Mary Lynn Rajskub, who is called, by her mother, 'her promiscuous daughter'), an old maid who names all her stuffed animals, and is wooed by a slimy television actor turned acting coach named Truman Hope (William Baldwin), whose claim to fame is guest starring in a three episode arc of the notoriously mediocre military crime show *JAG*.

   The 85 minute film was produced by Jeremy Coon, the maker of *Napoleon Dynamite*, a cult classic comedy from 2004, although this film is not quite as funny, albeit a bit more touching. Palmer wrote the screenplay, and while comedy takes center stage in this film, I sense that Palmer's strength might actually be in serious, adult, dramatic films, for he possesses a keen understanding of human motivation. The soundtrack and cinematography are, by comparison, merely solid, as is director Chris Bowman's helming. But, the thing that makes the film work is the acting- Palmer straddles the line between compelling and goofy, and Vincent Caso, as a Laotian-American kid, has perhaps the best supporting role in the film, as a punk who eventually does right by Tracy, after letting the fat man wallow in his stupidity and the wrath of his criminal pals- who con Tracy into letting them rob the store, only to turn on him, then falsely accuse him of sexual abuse. This leads Tracy to getting fired by his boss, Mr. Grigoratus (Bruce McGill), and his landing a part in a cable tv sci fi movie, or series episode, as an alien that gets a death scene, that leads to Truman quipping that he could have done the role.

   At its best, the film makes use of such moments that happen in real life, are humorous, but often in a degrading way, and these things can only be attributed to Palmer's own real life experiences in writing the film. Among them are Tracy's and Helen's professional animus; Mr. Grigoratus's making all his employees 'assistant managers; Tracy's and Truman's going to attend a lecture called 'Beyond the Method,' given by actor Rutger Hauer, only to have Truman rope Tracy into giving him his own ticket for Truman's date; Tracy's binge eating- including a scene where he pouts in bed, then reaches under it for a box of donuts; and a funny scene where Truman and Peggy try to sponsor Tracy in a sex offender rehabilitation program, oblivious to the fact that this would be a de facto admission of his own guilt. All of these moments, individually, are not much, but, taken as a whole, they make *Humble Pie* a bit more than its meager parts. Is it a great film? Is it a great comedy? No, on both scores. But it is better than expected, even as so much of it is expected, given its setups and denouements as an archetypal 'independent film comedy.' *Humble Pie* would be a bit much if one had too much of it, but in an 85 minute slice it's just right, with all apologies to Baby Bear.

DVD Review Of *The Graduate*
Copyright © by Dan Schneider, 2009

   Comedian Mike Nichols, in the mid-1960s, abandoned a flourishing comedy career with his partner, Elaine May, to become a filmmaker. His first film was the 1966 Elizabeth Taylor-Richard Burton vehicle *Who's Afraid Of Virginia Woolf?* His second, in 1967, was *The Graduate*- a film that, along with *Midnight Cowboy*, *Bonnie And Clyde*, and *Easy Rider*, ushered in mainstream Hollywood studios into the new era of director-centered cinema. Like many films that are landmark, for the external significance they bear, *The Graduate* has almost always been lauded as a great film. It's not. It's a good film that is more innovative than great, but which misses greatness for the simplest reason most films do- a screenplay that fails.

   The plot of the film is rather simple. Recent college graduate, Benjamin Braddock (Dustin Hoffman) returns to Los Angeles, after years at an Eastern university. On his first night back, at a party for him, the wife of his father's business partner, Mrs. Robinson (Anne Bancroft), whose first name Ben never utters, and the audience never finds out, seduces Ben. He escapes without consummation of the seduction, but shortly thereafter, calls her up to meet him at a local hotel, and an affair begins. The affair goes on for a few months, until Mrs. Robinson's daughter, Elaine (Katharine Ross), comes home from college. Ben's parents (William Daniels and Elizabeth Wilson), and Mr. Robinson (Murray Hamilton), force the kids to go out on a date, much to Mrs. Robinson's jealous chagrin. Ben finds out he likes Elaine, after initially trying to brush her off by taking her to a strip club (a precursor to the porno film scene in *Taxi Driver*, save that Ben does his deed deliberately), where a stripper's nipple pasties' bangles look like they are drumming Elaine's head. They plan a second date, and Mrs. Robinson forbids it, threatening to tell her daughter of her affair with Ben. He races to her room to tell her first, and Elaine ends things with Ben. Then, after just two dates, Ben thinks he's in love and resolves to pursue Elaine, even back to her college at UC- Berkeley. Nowadays, he'd be considered a stalker, and there are some funny scenes between Ben and Elaine, as well as Ben and his landlord, Mr. McCleery (Norman Fell, who's find stardom himself, a decade later in the tv sitcom *Three's Company*). Creeley thinks Ben's a radical, and wants to toss him out after Mr. Robinson calls Ben a degenerate for having slept with his wife. Ben soon finds out that Elaine is scheduled to marry a blond WASPy guy named Carl Smith, and decides to interrupt the wedding. He arrives too late, as they are just married. Nonetheless, he bangs on a church window, and Elaine rushes to be with him. Mrs. Robinson slaps her daughter twice, stating that it's too late, and Elaine disagrees. It's likely that she knows, as her mother told Ben earlier, that the only reason the Robinsons are together is because Mrs. Robinson got pregnant with Elaine. The two then fight off the others, and lock them inside the church with a cross to seal the doors. They hop on a bus and the film ends.

   The basic problem is that the film is really good, pushing near greatness, until Elaine finds out of the affair. She and Ben have only gone out once, and just on their second date, he seems to obsess over her, despite the reality of their having little in common. The love story that ensues is thus forced, and a bit pathetic, on the parts of both the parties. All the wacky adventures and musical montages (great as musical set pieces) do nothing to regain the wit, charm, and sophistication the film had when it chronicled Ben's and Mrs. Robinson's affair. In that portion of the film, the art of cinema is virtuosic- from camera angles to editing to dialogue to framing, and on and on. One particular scene has Ben's father confront him over his indolence, as Ben lolls in the family pool. The father blocks out the literal sun, just as his entreaty aims to block out his biological son. Just brilliant, and the film is suffused with these moments, plus the sublime music of *Simon*

And Garfunkel, timed to film so perfectly that, even more than the musical *films of The Beatles* and *The Monkees*, acts as a precursor to the MTV generation. Yet, after Elaine's discovery, the film goes from a comic version of a John Cassavetes film to a slightly above average Hollywood love story. As a viewer having never sen the full film, only its iconic moments, I was heartened to see how good the first two thirds of the film were, but the letdown at film's end only becomes that much more of a disappointment.

While the film became iconic, and a smash hit, looking back on it today, it seems tame-socially (not artistically). All the major players are what would have been called Rockefeller Republicans. And while the film's 'daring' approach to sex may have been the initial draw, it's likely that its rather 'safe' tale accounts for its enduring grace in the high opinion critics still have of it. The film garnered seven Academy Award nominations: Best Picture, Best Actor (Dustin Hoffman), Best Actress (Anne Bancroft), Best Supporting Actress (Katharine Ross), Best Adapted Screenplay (Calder Willingham and Buck Henry), and Best Cinematography, and Best Director, which is the only award it won, for Mike Nichols.

The DVD, put out by MGM, is a 40th Anniversary edition. A second disk is a 4 song CD, including *The Sound Of Silence*, *Mrs. Robinson*, Scarbourough *Fair/Canticle*, and *April Come She Will*, by *Simon And Garfunkel*. The first disk has the 105 minute long film in pristine condition, and a 2.35:1 aspect ratio. There are several worthy featurettes: *Students Of The Graduate*, *The Seduction*, *One On One With Dustin Hoffman* (an interview), and *The Graduate At 25*. There is also the original theatrical trailer. The film also has two audio commentaries, There is one with director Mike Nichols, one where he basically is queried by filmmaker Steven Soderbergh, and a second one with actors Dustin Hoffman and Katharine Ross. Both have pluses and minuses. The Nichols-Soderbergh track often descends into insider speak between the two filmmakers- not only in regards to the film, but in inside references between the two men, who are obviously friends. On the positive side, Nichols does hit upon the most important motivation in the film- anger. Specifically, he focuses on the anger Mrs. Robinson has toward the cosmos, for whatever grievances she feels the butt of. But, anger veins through all of the main characters- Mr. Robinson is angry over his loveless marriage, Elaine is angry over something that is not named, but seems far deeper than the rather wan 'betrayal' of a boy she's only gone out on one date with. But, Ben's rage suffuses the whole film. Online, there are a number of film trailer mashups on *The Graduate*, which portray Ben as off-kilter, psychologically bent, or a full blown stalker, and they are more on the money than they are humorous. No, Ben is not a budding serial killer, nor even a sociopath, but his rage has no focus, and inevitably, it will likely turn inward. In fact, as much of a letdown as the second half of the film is, it is realistic in the sense that it shows Ben doing all he can to screw up his life. Film critic Roger Ebert, who wildly praised the film in 1967, gave a much better and more sober assessment of the film in 1997:

Today, looking at 'The Graduate,' I see Benjamin not as an admirable rebel, but as a self-centered creep whose put-downs of adults are tiresome. (Anyone with average intelligence should have known, in 1967, that the word 'plastics'' contained valuable advice--especially valuable for Benjamin, who lacks creative instincts and is destined to become a corporate drudge.) Mrs. Robinson is the only person in the movie who is not playing old tapes. She is bored by a drone of a husband, she drinks too much, she seduces Benjamin not out of lust but out of kindness or desperation. Makeup and lighting are used to make Anne Bancroft look older (she was 36 when the movie was made, and Hoffman was 30). But there is a scene where she is drenched in a rainstorm; we can see her face clearly and without artifice, and she is a great beauty. She is also sardonic, satirical and articulate--the only person in the movie you would want to have a conversation with.

Well, not really, since the conversation she and Ben have of art, during their affair, shows that Mrs. Robinson is no great conversationalist, but Ebert's point that she is a bit more weighty than the other characters is correct. In short, Mrs. Robinson is the only character who would have been at home in a John Cassavetes film, that is, a film for adults, and one could easily see Gena Rowlands essaying the part. Yet, Nichols also fetishizes his film a bit too much, crowing to Soderbergh that the critics missed a moment in the first hotel room sequence between Ben and Mrs. Robinson, where, in preparation for her arrival, Ben stows some condoms in the night table. Well, the reason is because it occurs so briefly, and the camera is too far from the condoms to be able to make out what it is Ben tucks away, not because there was a critical lapse. The Hoffman-Ross track has some good observations and reminiscences, but too many silent spots where nothing at all is said. Hoffman attempts to speak on the innovative nature of the film, and this is true, as it is far more truly innovative stylistically (with POV shots through Mrs. Robinson's legs, or through statue openings, and brilliant edits that switch between locations seamlessly) than Jean-Luc Godard's imitative *Breathless*.

The film's ending, while a narrative failure, considering the film's beginning, is an interesting commentary on the shallowness of American life (then and now), as it celebrates the shallow (Ben's and Elaine's 'relationship'), the idea that mere persistence ends up with reward, and that other people's desires are meaningless. And, at film's end, Ben is in no better emotional and psychological shape than he was at film's start, save that he now has a mate to share in his anomy. There is also the sinking feeling that these two people will end up, in a few years, just like their parents, for they have rebelled against nothing but easy opportunity and privileges that the real rebels of their era were actually fighting to get. Would it have been too much for Nichols to insert another great montage (used elsewhere at 'transition' moments in the film and life of Ben) showing us Elaine's and Ben's romance over a few months, or even weeks, before getting to the scene where Mrs. Robinson 'outs' herself? Because the film, and especially its end, is so shallow- see the early scene where one of Ben's dad's friends tries to excite Ben with the concept of 'plastics' as a buzzword- the film has nothing that penetrates the way that truly great films do.

The Graduate is a good film that spoke to its time, but offers little that can be related to nowadays- at least not without a knowing nod to its kitschiness. Yes, it's light years above contemporary Hollywood tripe, but that alone does not make it great. Nor do the boasts of many bad filmmakers who cite this film, flawed as it is, as a seminal influence on them when they do not even come close to its overrated heights, in terms of quality nor content, mean much to the art in the actual film. Despite that, it is a good film, and a funny film. In fact, it is its comedic elements which make the film still appealing to watch, whereas its dramatic ones have wizened. Then again, it's sometimes better to avoid the grown ups' table when the kids have much better desserts. As Ben Braddock, and he'll testify to that.

Film Review Of *Tora! Tora! Tora!*
Copyright © by Dan Schneider, 2013

The 1970 144 minute long color film, *Tora! Tora! Tora!*, a joint production of Hollywood and Japan, has often been slagged on by critics as being bloated and dull, and while it is not a great epic film, it is a faithful and well made film depicting the attack on Pearl Harbor, on December 7th, 1941. The decision to film the American and Japanese parts in their native language was a breakthrough for the day, and adds to the realism, although the unbordered white subtitles are often washed out against the white military uniforms of the Japanese commanders. There are some impressive effects sequences, and air battles, and some poor model work, as well as poor matte screen usage, and rear projection scenes, but overall one does feel one is in the middle of battle, and the film, overall, is much better than the later, bloated faux epic, *Pearl Harbor*. There are also a few scenes shot on soundstages that do a poor job of representing ships' interiors, and the use of model ships in soundstage pools, with unscaled water, is also a minor giveaway of old time special effects, but that is not the only marker that this film is one of the last of its kind. Midway through the film, at about the 55% mark, there is an intermission, which is a clear indicator that, even though this film was made in 1970, it is a product of the old Hollywood studio system. One need only watch the film's trailer for this to become obvious, as well.

Tora! Tora! Tora! is shot in a 2.35:1 aspect ratio, and was directed by Richard Fleischer, Kinji Fukasaku, and Toshio Masuda, with cinematography by Charles F. Wheeler, Osamu Furuya, Sinsaku Himeda, and Masamichi Satoh, from a screenplay by Larry Forrester, Ryuzo Kikushima, and Hideo Oguni, adapted from the books *Tora! Tora! Tora!*, by Gordon W. Prange, and *The Broken Seal*, by Ladislas Farago. The soundtrack, by Jerry Goldsmith is rather non-notable, and not one of his better works. Perhaps the best technical job done in the film is the editing together of the American and Japanese halves of the film, by editors Pembroke J. Herring, Chikaya Inoue, and James E. Newcom. Not well known is that famed Japanese film legend Akira Kurosawa adapted parts of the Japanese story part of the screenplay, and also was responsible for several scenes that were shot, before he was removed from the film.

Nonetheless, the film is informative, well acted, and rather interesting to watch, even though the outcome of that attack, and the war that followed it are and were all well known at the time of the film's making. But, that's because the film is not meant to be straight drama, rather a police procedural on a crime, this one a war crime. We see the Japanese ambivalence, arrogance, and stupidity, even as we see the American arrogance, sloth, and bureaucratic incompetence. There have been numerous minor factual inaccuracies reported in the film for decades, from the designs of warships to whether or not Admiral Yamamoto actually uttered the words that end the film: '*I fear all we have done is to awaken a sleeping giant and fill him with a terrible resolve.*' Of course, none of this really matters, as long as the big picture is correct, for it was filmdom that gifted us with the notion that one should always print the legend!

That stated, this film is remarkably evenhanded, and does not make caricatures nor stereotypes out of either side. The film opens with Japan's Axis Pact agreement with Germany and Italy, and then careers down to the last 35 or so minutes being the actual attack, which catches most of the American military unawares, save for a few wise Cassandras. The amazing thing about the American response is that they have cracked the Japanese military code and can know more quickly than the Japanese Ambassador in Washington D.C. what the Japanese government is doing, and they STILL arrogantly think the Japanese will not dare attack, or if they do, it will be elsewhere, other than Pearl

Harbor. The Japanese, however, have planned well, and know that an early Sunday morning attack will be the best, yet, they are not wholly successful, because their main targets, most of the American aircraft carriers, are out at sea on maneuvers.

The three main characters of the film, wherein the absence of A List Hollywood and Japanese stars, is noticeable, are Admiral Yamamoto (Soh Yamamura), Col. Rufus Bratton (E.G. Marshall), and Lt. Commander Alvin Kramer (Wesley Addy). One almost senses that if these three men were the ones in charge of their nations, at least the Pacific Theater of the Second World War would never have been waged. Other characters of note include Admiral Husband Kimmel (Martin Balsam), Secretary of State Cordell Hull (George Macready), Secretary of War Henry Stimson (Joseph Cotton), Admiral William Halsey (James Whitmore), and Lt. General Walter Short (Jason Robards). That the film elects to never show an actor portraying President Franklin Delano Roosevelt is a good choice, for nothing that the President's underlings state, at least in regards to the sneak attack, could have been better elucidated coming from the President's mouth. Oddly, so many things went wrong, especially on the American side, that, had the film not been depicting history, one might have claimed it tritely written, for having to follow the Dumbest Possible Action trope; a term not invented until a decade later, during the rise of the subgenre of slasher horror films.

Overall, though, *Tora! Tora! Tora!* is a good film to watch, and one of the better films about World War Two ever made. While it's true that, cinematically, it cannot compete with a superb biographical film like Patton, in it slack of a compelling central character, this is the rare film that benefits from a lack of character exposition, and a focus on plot elements, since, in essence, the main character if the place of Pearl Harbor, on that historic day, at that historic moment. Human characters become mere plot devices, as the idea of narrative inverts itself to open up the past. On this level, the film is a resounding success, even as it may merely be adequate on all other levels. There are worse fates for a work of art to have.

DVD Review Of *Being There*
Copyright © by Dan Schneider, 2010

Hal Ashby made a series of quirky films in the 1970s that were highly regarded, then succumbed to a drug addiction and died before the 1980s were through. The most famous of these were *Harold And Maude, Shampoo, Coming Home*, and *Being There*. Almost all of his films, however, are products of their times, thus do not hold up well to more modern viewers. *Harold And Maude* was a farce about a 'romance between a young man and an old woman, *Shampoo* was a vehicle for Warren Beatty in between more serious films, and *Coming Home* was a rather standard anti-Vietnam tract that, in light of films like *Apocalypse Now, The Deer Hunter*, and *Full Metal Jacket*, has little bite. Of the four most famous films mentioned, though, *Being There* is the least dated of the films. And this is because of two factors: first is that it starred Peter Sellers. Enough said. The second is that later films, most notably *Rain Man* and *Forrest Gump*, expanded upon the themes this film did, and a) made them more mainstream while b) watering them down to the point that they merely became gawkfests for the retards the film centered upon.

While *Being There* is nowhere near a great film, it is several cuts above its predecessors in this genre, mainly because it does not overtly tug at one's heartstrings. The film is, in a sense, based upon a singular conceit: that a retarded man can succeed in life by the even greater ignorance of the non-retarded. It does require an immense degree of suspension of disbelief, but if one accepts that premise, this slight movie does have its charms. It opens with the morning routine of a man named Chance (Sellers), who works as a gardener on a rich estate. He is addicted to television, to the point that he often mimics what he sees onscreen. One morning, while eating his breakfast, the black maid, Louise (Ruth Attaway), who runs the estate tells him that the Old Man (the estate's owner) is dead. Chance has little reaction, and is berated by the maid, who eventually leaves and hugs him goodbye. Chance is then informed that he must vacate the premises by an attorney handling the deceased man's will. Chance does not know what to make of this, and we never learn anything of his background, although he is clearly a man in his 50s. If he is related to the dead man is a mystery. The only hint of his past comes from the maid, who, later in the film, after Chance gains fame, claims that she raised him since he was a boy.

Newly homeless, Chance wanders through Washington, D.C., near where his residence was. His attire- that of the Old man- suggests that he is wealthy, and he has a series of comic encounters with mostly black people. Seeing himself on a television monitor in an electronics store window, he tries to use the remote control he carries to change the picture. He backs up into the street, where his leg is injured by a backing up limousine. The woman, named Eve Rand (Shirley MacLaine), seeks to avoid a lawsuit from Chance, whom she assumes to be wealthy, so offers to bring him home so her private doctor (Richard A. Dysart) can look after him. Her husband, Ben Rand (Melvyn Douglas), is also under doctor's care, suffering from aplastic anemia. They have a whole wing of their mansion converted to a hospital ward. All involved have mistaken his being Chance the Gardener for having the name Chauncey Gardner. Whenever Chance tells of his plight, such as being forced from his home, it is misinterpreted as his being forced out of business by the government. As Ben and Chance recover they become friends, and Eve, much younger than Ben, starts to fall for Chance, as both assume his conservative demeanor that of breeding, not simplemindedness. His real descriptions of gardens and his tending to them are interpreted as homilies about American business.

Through his friendship with Ben, Chance gets to meet the President Of The United States, (Jack Warden), who likewise mistakes Chance's simplicity for depth, and quotes from him in a speech. This makes Chance an overnight media sensation, whisked to fancy parties and the talk show circuit, where his simple ideas are taken to be wisdom in the emergent sound bite era. Reporters and the President want to know all they can find out about Chance, aka Chauncey Gardner. When nothing turns up (recapping the diegetic problem proffered to the viewer), people assume Chance's past is a mystery, and that the FBI or CIA are behind it. This only further makes Chance seem important. The misassumptions pile up, and Eve throws herself at Chance, who, while watching a love scene on tv, mimics it, until it's over. This confuses Eve, who takes his utterances to mean that he wants her to masturbate for him, as he watched the Edward G. Robinso gangster film, *Little Casear*. She does, and ascribes her orgasm to Chance's wisdom. Throughout the film, only Rand's doctor comes to learn the truth of Chance's past (what little there is), but since he sees no harm in it, and Chance seems to have ameliorated his clients' lives, he says nothing; even when Rand tacitly pushes his wife and Chance together, and makes preparations for Chance to ascend to a high place in his corporation.

Ben soon dies, with the doctor and Chance at his side. At his funeral, the President gives a dull hagiography of Rand, as the pallbearers whisper about potential replacements for the President. As Ben's coffin is to be interred in the family mausoleum, they unanimously agree on Chauncey Gardner as the man for the job. Meanwhile, Chance wanders off during the President's speech, and fixes a small sapling, then contentedly walks on the surface of a lake, stops, dips his umbrella into the lake, as th e President utters the bon mot, 'Life is a state of mind.' This lone moment of supernaturalism, or magical realism, has led many critics to imbue meanings into the film that take it into the wildly metaphysical. Most of these are truly silly, for the ending is meant to be ambiguous, meaning that many ends are possible, but none is definite. In a deeper, more serious film this could be a problem. In a small, simple film, it helps floriate its earlier scenes into a bit more. Not much more, but a bit. It also helps to demarcate that the pretension resides not in the film, its director, nor its ending, but in the critics of same, thus neatly recapitulating the same errors that propel the film's lead character through it.

The DVD, by Warner Brothers, is bare bones, and has only the 130 minute, color film, in a 1.78:1 aspect ratio. There is no audio commentary, only the original theatrical trailer, and a featurette called *Memories From Being There*, which has reminiscences about the film. Overall, a too skimpy package. As for the film? The screenplay is solid, adapted by Jerzy Kosinski from his same titled novel, with the help of Robert C. Jones. It makes good use of ambient audio and video, such as vintage era commercials from television, which give the viewer an idea of what is present in Chance's mind. There is also excellent scoring by Johnny Mandel, especially in his use of classical music, especially pieces by Erik Satie, and Richard Strauss's *Also Sprach Zarathustra*, most filmically famed from Stanley Kubrick's 1968 film, *2001: A Space Odyssey*. The acting is first rate. MacLaine is solid, in a slight role, and Sellers has brilliant moments, and Douglas actually deserved his Best Supporting Actor Academy Award, for he actually acts, and does not preen, like Robert Duvall's fun, but slight, turn in Francis Ford Coppola's *Apocalypse Now*, released the same year. Caleb Deschanel's cinematography is solid but unspectacular.

The film's weakest moments occur when Chance is with Eve, for her sexual come-ons seem forced and from a different film, as does the narrative of the President's impotence with his wife. Also, the film is not really a satire nor black comedy. It is more in line with the old time comedies of manner, for it is far more subtle than a satire, which would have made the idea of Chance's being a blank slate for others' expectations something to ram down the throat of the viewer. But, the film always restrains itself from that temptation, much in the same way that Martin Scorsese's film, *The King Of Comedy*, would do just a few years later. And, like Being There, that film is also often mislabeled. But, while

Being There is not the sort of film, like the aforementioned Kubrick and Coppola films, that will leave on endlessly buzzing over its meaning, Being There is an enjoyable film whose minor pleasures can only grow in the mind, just as Chance would claim. Just, lay off too much of the manure many of the bad critics pack it with, ok?

Film Review Of *Star Trek* (2009)
Copyright © by Dan Schneider, 2011

I have never been a great *Star Trek* fan- never a Trekkie, Trekker, nor any other variant, although I have seen almost all the film versions in the franchise's history, and most of the television episodes of the assorted series. That said, each of the television series after the original 1960s version, seemed to get worse. *The Next Generation* was a pale imitation of the first show, and not a single trio of characters in it, or subsequent series, had the realistic male bonding repartee Kirk, McCoy, and Spock had in the original. Also, history shows us that technology gets smaller and sleeker with each generation, thus, ironically, the fiscally challenged simplicity of the 1960s show has always been more 'futuristic' and accurate a representation of things than the Byzantine technology later films and series have indulged in. *Deep Space 9* was too static a setting and its political symbolism too ham-fisted. *Voyager* came the closest to the original show, in that it had an often lone starship facing the unknown, while *Enterprise* was an abomination- poorly written, acted, and wholly superfluous, since all the other shows came later and we knew things would turn out ok. In some ways, the 1970s animated series was the best sequel series, with the original characters on adventures similar to the original show's. As for all prior movies? A few entertaining films, but mostly bloated television episodes, and bad ones, at that. Still, a handful of shows in each episode reached the first show's magic.

With J.J. Abrams' 2009 film, which I streamed from Netflix, well, they weren't even trying any longer. With cuts every 5-6 seconds there's virtually no time to build character nor any real plot, the actors all do caricatures of the original roles, mannerisms over emoting, and anyone coming to this as a stand alone film, with no knowledge of the prior history, would be utterly lost. The cavalcade of absurdity begins with the fact that this is all set in a different universe than the prior series' timelines are, thus it is wholly disconnected. Amazingly, many dense fans don't even get this fact, although characters state it is an alternate timeline in an omniverse and, logically (to paraphrase a Vulcan), the term alternate necessarily implies at least two different things. Then there is the comic interpretation of most characters: Kirk's hand swell to immense size, Scotty is a retard with an alien sidekick, and is beamed into the Enterprise's sewer system, Chekhov (Anton Yelchin) is a teenaged Wesley Crusher (get the reference?) wannabe with a Russian lisp, and Uhura (Zoe Saldana) and Spock (Zachary Quinto) are, respectively, a sex goddess and horn dog- oh, and they're lovers. The only characters even remotely like their television counterparts are Captain Christopher Pike (Bruce Greenwood), Doctor McCoy (Karl Urban), and Mr. Sulu (John Cho).

There really is no story. Somehow, the tv universe Spock (yes, played by Leonard Nimoy) has come to this alternate timeline after the Romulan home planet is destroyed. He is followed through a black hole by a Romulan named Nero (one of seemingly endless earth baddies' names recycled for films) who amazingly can destroy worlds, and does so to Vulcan. How this tv Romulan (and they were like Vulcans, not bald, tattooed cyberpunks on tv) got such a weapon is unknown since the tv Romulans never had anything nearly as powerful. This ends up killing Kirk's father, and leaving alternate Kirk (Chris Pine) an often who grows up rambunctious and, after cheating on exams, stowing aboard Pike's Enterprise, and generally screwing everything up, miraculously becomes captain in a few hours, defeats the inept Nero (Eric Bana), who is trying to destroy Earth, as he did Vulcan, and is hailed as a hero.

There are so many implausibilities- scientific and common sense-wise, in the plot written by Roberto Orci and Alan Kurtzman, that to recount them is a waste of time. This 127 minute long film really isn't a movie (or this movie really isn't a film- take your pick), but a wannabe video game or music video, or both, merged into some incredibly dull 'scenes' that, truth be told, I don't even recall. It's that ephemeral a thing. The scoring, by Michael Giacchino is similarly inept. Music is scary when nothing onscreen is. It's pulsepounding when there is nothing pulsepounding, and when it's not lamely trying to provoke reactions its banally restating the obvious feelings the images evoke. The cinematography, such as it is, by Daniel Mindel, is a yawn since it is mostly computer graphics, anyway. In short, this film isn't just bad Star Trek, but bad cinema. Granted, if you are familiar with the *Star Trek* mythos you'll enjoy a few moments that play off longstanding character points, as well as the chance to gaze at the gorgeous Zoe Saldana, but once the points are made and your boner has subsided, you are still left with a bad film, and one which you know, despite this being an alternate universe, not a thing will go bad in the ship Kirk commands. The film lacks drama for in order to have drama one needs to build expectation, and since the film never pauses- from the first seconds of the film, begun in medias res, to reflect, this is nigh impossible.

Yet, despite many critical plaudits, and despite many bad critics calling this film a space opera, it is neither. It is simply a trifle. A sleek shiny trifle, but one with nothing under the hood, as there is no engine. The speed you think it's been going is all rear projection. You are still. You are motionless. You realize that you are not where you thought you were. You are in a place of imagination (sort of). You are in a world of substance and shadow, things and ideas, that's the signpost up ahead. Next stop....*The Twilight Zone.* Ok, so I mixed up classic television science fiction series. But that's what a fan of the *Star Trek* franchise will feel- a slight but then growing alienation, for this film is an utterly generic sci fi/action film- one with a few mildly entertaining moments, but nothing more. It is not even a mildly entertaining genre film, much less film overall. It has been utterly rent and denatured of all its *Star Trek*ness. As for the rest of the intelligent filmgoers? Give'em 20, 25 minutes, tops, and they'll be flipping through scenes at the touch of a thumb. *Go for it!*

Review of *My Father, The Genius*
Copyright © by Dan Schneider, 2011

Documentaries on individuals often fall short of the mark because of a tendency to hagiographize or demonize. Rare is the documentary that cuts it straight down the middle. Lucia Small's 2002 documentary, *My Father, The Genius*, does not go down the middle, but comes fairly close, although I have some quibbles with it. That stated, it's a very good portrait of her own father, Glen Howard Small, an influential architect who has never quite received his due from his peers, mostly because of his inability to brink the bullshit concomitant to most business relationships.

For this he should be admired, as well for his being at least three decades ahead of the curve on environmental designs of buildings. Yes, some of his early works, such as the Biomorphic Biosphere and Green Machine, reeks of the Utopian lunacy of the 1960s, and, in practice, well, could never really be put in to practice because of its impracticality (many architects, including Small's 'God'- Frank Lloyd Wright- fell into this trap) and its aesthetic lack. The film also delves in to the man's less savory side. Aside from an inability to brink bullshit, Small comes off as a man with little ability to be honest with his family, even as he demands public honesty from business associates. He seems to have been a serial womanizer, had two families that he abandoned, then complains how the women did not understand him. Yes, it's clear that they would likely not understand him since he married and slept with women who were not architects nor on his intellectual level. Hence he created his own hell, and subjected the five kids he had, from the two marriages, to untold pains.

Frankly, I would have preferred to not have been exposed to this side of the man. Why? If Leonardo da Vinci were cruel to stray dogs, or if Ludwig Van Beethoven had a thing for underaged girls, would either of these things diminished their work? Granted, one can see why Lucia Small, who did the film after a request from her father to write his biography, would find her father's personal lacks a subject worth delving in to, but to the objective watcher? Not really, especially since her father so clearly fits in to the stereotype of the creator as misunderstood genius, braying against the benighted set, and then showing him up to be an asshole, on a personal level. It merely perpetuates a stereotype (the artistic genius is an asshole cliché) that artists of depth and quality (such as myself and others I know) have to thresh through, unnecessarily. But, I could take it more, in this 83 minute long film, id the daughter had actually shown more of her father's work. Given the film's title, I think she could have let us make up our own mind as to whether or not Glenn Small is a genius. As is, we see precious little of the completed buildings he has designed. All we get are the talking heads of friends and enemies of Small's who praise or damn him for various incidents and qualities he has endured or possesses.

The film follows the man for a couple of years, it seems, and flashes back to home movies (those with Glen behind the camera inevitably show landscapes and architecture, not people, we are informed), talking heads, and Glen bitching about this or that. Interestingly, in looks, demeanor, and attitude, Glen reminds me much of my own natural father, who lived in Southern California, especially in his own stymied emotions and lack of empathy toward others. The difference is that my father took the easy way out in life, whereas Glen does not. And, eventually, Glen (after some time living with his oldest daughter) moves away from the Los Angeles area, and up to Oregon, to be a 'big fish in a small pond,' as he calls and enjoys it.

The film does show, though, that the architectural world is like almost all others in business and the arts (since architecture encompasses elements of both this is no real surprise) in its failure to actually reward quality, because, as Glen rightly points out, from the little we see of his work, had many of his buildings seen the light of day he likely would be a national icon, like Antoni Gaudi is in Spain. Instead, he has been blackballed, literally, being fired from a school (the Southern California Institute of Architecture- Sci-Arc) he co-founded, after promises of tenure, and figuratively, from magazines that showcase more conventional work from lesser lights.

In a number of reviews of the film, Glen is quoted as stating that he wishes the film focused more on his work and less on his personal life, and all the critics take this as proof of his narcissism. Clearly, few critics ever thumb through dictionaries because the statement is in no way narcissistic, and, as I mentioned the same flaw in the film earlier, it merely shows that Glen was able to get this flaw, too. This flaw is also why many reviews of the film propound variations of this meme: *When famed but failed architect Glen Howard Small drew up his will, he requested that the middle daughter of his first, somewhat estranged, family should write his biography.* The whole point of the film is that Small is NOT famed and NOT a failure! The flaw in the film is that it fails to emphasize this point clearly enough, thus we never get to judge whether or not another cliché about Glen is true or not: that he's a 'self proclaimed genius.' Nonetheless, the film gives enough to entertain and enlighten one about the man, his family, and his past. Glen Small may never be held in the esteem that Wright and Gaudi are, but that does not mean he was not as good. If only the film allowed me the certainty of that claim.

Review Of *The One Percent*
Copyright © by Dan Schneider, 2011

Jamie Johnson's 2006 documentary *The One Percent* is an amateurish, but important, documentary because Johnson, heir to the Johnson & Johnson mega-fortune, uses his financial connections to a) get interviews with notoriously wealthy and condescending scions and entrepreneurs, and b) elicits some of the true condescension and loathing the upper classes have for the working and impoverished classes. The editing, dialectic, and statistics shown are rather obvious, and much of the film comes off as guilty white liberal über-rich guilt; especially scenes with poor and minority people; often playing into the condescending Wise Negro Noble Savage stereotypes. On the other hand, Johnson interview with the soon to be dead laissez-faire and Trickle Down economist and fraud Milton Friedman is priceless, as it shows how out of touch with reality and delusional the old fool was. Too bad he did not live a few years longer to see almost all his theorizing proven to be garbage, with the resurrection of Keynesian economic reality. For the few moments of Friedman on film, alone, Johnson's film can be forgiven its otherwise significant flaws; including Johnson's own stilted, poorly written, and leaden narration.

Others who are interviewed include Robert Reich, Adnan Khashoggi, Bill Gates Sr., and Steve Forbes- as delusional as he ever was. The other revelation in the film is the interview clips with Adnan Khashoggi, who comes across, despite his reputation, as surprisingly realistic about the inequalities of life. Most of the people interviewed, however- be it European playboys (a studly Italian baron who stays at hotels not because they are chic but because he likes being served) or self starting multi-millionaires, or the people who run seminars to teach the scions of such people how to protect their wealth, are remarkably (if not predictably) out of touch with reality, and downright scornful of the have nots of the world.

Other than documenting the obvious wealth gap in America, and the world, Johnson also charts his own personal story, including the tensions his film has on his wealthy clan. His father, who once bankrolled a film on South African apartheid and the American companies that benefited from it (Including Johnson & Johnson), is now loath to speak of wealth, because after his own film made it to PBS he was kneecapped by the major shareholders of the company. Johnson's mother, on the other hand, who married into money, fully supports Johnson's film, while lesser members of the clan share varying degrees of revulsion to his project. As the film progresses, we see bits of the elder Johnson's film, and think we are going to see him emerge as a fully formed and decent human being, only to slip back into and under his masque of cowardly silence. Another interesting trope of the film, and perhaps the most interesting other than the exposing of Friedman's intellectual bankruptcy, is what a bastard Warren Buffett is, despite his currying media favor by coming out for higher taxes on the rich and giving his fortune away, for, when he finds out his granddaughter is appearing in Johnson's film he cuts her off and denies there relation, a mini-scandal some years back.

As for the film's flaws, they lie with the all too real but all too non-revelatory segments on poverty-stricken Caribbean sugar workers in Florida, whose work and entry into the U.S. are subsidized by the federal government, which artificially inflates U.S. sugar prices, and poor Chicago residents being gentrified out of their neighborhoods, as well as a particularly saccharine scene where a none too bright black cab driver propounds the worst sorts of clichés about true riches being love and family, and Johnson letting him blather on embarrassingly. There are some funny moments, such as when the Johnson family financial advisor whines and calls Johnson a spoiled 'trustafarian;' a cool play on the Rastafarian term.

On a purely technical level, the film is a mess: poorly edited, wandering camera angles, poorly focused, and the narrative arcs never quite cohere. *The One Percent*, as a film, does have value, but that is mainly based upon its maker's ability to get access into areas where other filmmakers could never go, whereas its content is rather banal (and banally presented); however correct. Still, on the whole, while a subject like this would seem to be something an Errol Morris could work wonders on, one must give credit where it is warranted; Jamie Johnson has balls and a soul. That may not be enough to earn one the sobriquet of artist, but it surely does earn him the label *mensch*. Would that the many members of the male sex that he interviews in the film were equally worthy of that title and we might have a world where such a film would be obviated. Ah, perchance....

DVD Review of *The Magician*
Copyright © by Dan Schneider, 2010

Ingmar Bergman's black and white, 101 minute long, 1958 film, *The Magician* (*Ansiktet*, or *The Face*), is a rare film for a number of reasons. First, it is rare for being a comedy, a drama, a melodrama, a psychodrama, and a horror film. Second, it is rare for excelling at all these formats, although not strongly enough in any one of them to push the envelope of greatness. Third, despite this, it is an excellent film, and rare because it is so undervalued on its own merits, and as a work in the canon of an acknowledged master of cinema. Fourth, it is rare because there is a dissonance in the acting performance of the film's lead, Max Von Sydow (who plays Albert Emanuel Vogler, a con artist carny- who wears false facial hair and a wig as part of his act), and all of the rest of the actors in the film who, while all competent, never shine as brightly as they do in other roles- and all are Bergman stock actors.

Not so rare is the fact that most critics, then and now, utterly whiff on what is important in the film. Most try to paint the film as the self-portrait of an artist (i.e.- Bergman on Bergman) when this is clearly not the case. The film is, however, a biting satire and debunking of the mid-19th Century novelty of Spiritualism. The idea that Vogler is a stand-in for Bergman, even to the point that the film's (literally and figuratively) 'sunny ending' is Bergman's revenge on his critics is puerile, at worst, and insipid, at best. First, the Vogler character is simply not an artist. He is an entertainer, and the lowest grade of such. To claim that a spiritualist mesmerist is an artist is akin to claiming that professional wrestlers are artists, as well.

The film opens up with a surprisingly similar setup to John Ford's *Stagecoach*, with people on board a coach and headed toward hostile territory. The switch is that, in the Ford film, the hostilities lie in the hinterlands whereas in this film it is the civilized town that Vogler's troupe is headed to where the hostilities are lying in wait. It is 1846, and Vogler and his band are renowned on the Continent, as favorites of kings, and scourges of modern science, which views them as frauds, charlatans, and thieves. In the town they are entering, they are soon stopped by Police Chief Starbeck (Toivo Pawlo), whose men escort them to the home of Consul Egerman (Erland Josephson), who has requested this because he has a bet with Dr. Vergerus (Gunnar Björnstrand), the Minister of Health. Egerman believes that there are unknown powers in the world, and that Vogler may represent them. Vergerus denies this. They want to force Vogler to perform for them to settle their bet. Among those on Vogler's coach are his wife Manda (Ingrid Thulin)- who poses as Mr. Aman, Vogler's assistant, because the troupe has been on the lam from assorted local lawmen for some time; Granny Vogler (Naima Wifstrand)- who makes a fortune selling bogus potions; Tubal (Åke Fridell)- the troupe's impresario and wily financial manager; Simson (Lars Ekborg)- the coach driver: and Johan Spegel (Bengt Ekerot)- a dying actor they find in a swamp, bring with them, and who presumably dies on the coach.

Vergerus sets out to humiliate Vogler, who plays at being mute (it is 65 minutes into the film before Von Sydow utters a word), and degrades him with a physical examination. Then he instructs Egerman to let them sleep and eat in the servants' quarters. Down there, some ribald fun occurs between Tubal and the Consul's cook, the widow Sofia Garp (Sif Ruud), as well as Simson and a comely maid, Sara (Bibi Andersson). Meanwhile, upstairs, Egerman's wife, Ottilia Egerman (Gertrud Fridh) tries to seduce Vogler. She begs him to come to her bedroom at 2 am, stating that she and her husband have not been intimate since the death of their daughter, and she has drugged him to sleep. Egerman overhears this and tries to stay awake- then confronts his wife for her emotional betrayal, while Vogler is maddened by the hypocrisy he witnesses. In his world, he is a harmless entertainer, not a con man. A bit later, he is surprised to see Spegel, who put on a melodramatic death scene in the coach. Spegel announces he is a ghost, or thinks he is, and then really dies. His body is hidden by Vogler.

The next morning, the show goes on and Vogler and company help humiliate the Police Chief by hypnotizing his wife, who spills the beans on his perversions. When a trick with a servant goes wrong, the servant attacks Vogler and seemingly kills him. Declared dead by Vergerus, Starbeck orders an immediate autopsy. Vogler's troupe puts the body of Spegel in Vogler's place, and the autopsy is to be done in the attic. After nothing out of the ordinary is found, Starbeck leaves with his 'official' document, and Manda locks Vergerus in the attic with Spegel's body, and the living Vogler, who plays a psychological cat and mouse game with his would be tormentor- whom he overheard making a pass at Manda. He ends up stepping on Vergerus's eyeglasses and posing as an apparition. Presumably Vergerus never looked unde the towel covering the face of Spegel lest he'd never have fallen for this ruse- and it is minor plot points like this that prevent the film from reaching greatness. Having scared Vergerus, Manda puts an end to Vogler's revenge, and he then begs the Egermans and Vergerus for money for their performance, but Mrs. Egerman denies she knows him without his costume on. He and his troupe try to leave the Consul's grounds before the police are called back, but Tubal has decided to stay with Mrs. Garp, and Granny also decides to leave, for she has enough money to retire on. Sara, the maid, meanwhile, begs to come with them and Stimson, and while waiting for her the police stop and seemingly arrest the Voglers, even as the skies- stormy throughout the film, are now clear and sunny. But, it turns out they are not arrested, but informed that the King Of Sweden wants to see them perform later that day. The chastened non-believers beg the Voglers to not mention their little 'meeting.' The film abruptly ends with the light and song-filled departure of the Voglers' carriage.

Much of the film's imagery (see the attic scene where Vogler's hand extends from behind a barred wall and mirrors crack), psychology, and percussive drum beats would be totally stolen by Roman Polanski for his 1965 horror masterpiece *Repulsion*. The musical scoring is absolutely stellar- one of the best in all of Bergman's oeuvre, and Erik Nordgren deserves great credit for it. The cinematography, by Gunnar Fischer, especially in the forest and attic scenes, is magnificent. It would be his penultimate collaboration with Bergman, before Sven Nykvist became his cinematographer. Bergman wrote the screenplay, which he adapted from a G.K. Chesterton play called *Magic*. The acting is all good, but, as mentioned, Von Sydow shines above all others. This is most aptly shown, early on when Vogler, the consummate con man, is watching Spegel's claim of imminent death. When the man melodramatically expires, even the viewer wonders if it is so, for it seems unreal; yet clearly Vogler believes it, for he is stunned to later find Spegel is alive, thus underlining the claim that the easiest marks are often con artists themselves. As for the DVD, put out by The Criterion Collection, this is one of their weaker recent efforts, save for an almost pristine transfer of the film. First there are the standard Criterion white, unbordered subtitles on an often blanched screen, which makes for difficult reading, and worse- no English dubbed option, which should be de rigueur, considering the prices Criterion charges. Even worse is no audio commentary. By now, these should also be standard issue on all DVDs. Instead, all one gets is a brief video essay by film historian Peter Cowie, and two Bergman interviews- a short 1967 video interview and a 1990 audio interview, in English, conducted by film directors Olivier Assaya and Stig Bjorkman. Not even a theatrical trailer is included. As stated, a really poor set of 'extras.' There is also an insert booklet with an anomic essay by Assayas, a slightly better essay by film critic Geoff Andrew, and thoughts on the film from Bergman.

Like many others, Cowie, Assaya, and Andrew perpetuate the folly that this film somehow, along with being a self-portrait of Bergman, is in line with many of Bergman's other filmic treatises on death and divinity. But the evidence for this is simply non-existent in the film. Like the misconstrual of a carny fraud with an artist, these critics mistake a critique of the quest for reason with a de facto march on beliefs in God, or gods. Yet, nowhere, explicitly nor implicitly, in the film is this mentioned nor dramatized. In fact, only Mrs. Egerman even mentions God, and this only in her plaintive, and believable, beseechings to Vogler over the death of her daughter. But, most importantly is how disgusted Vogler is by her and her query, for he has no such interest in God. Instead, the actual target of the film is the human folly of self-deception. Without exception, every character given more than a throwaway line to speak deals with a self-deception of some sort: Vogler with his craft and marriage; Manda with her marriage; the Egermans with their marriage, Vergerus with his beliefs in science, Starbeck with his abuse of power, the Egermans' help with their own limitations and self-satisfactions, Tubal with his own honor, and Granny Vogler with her own desire to still commit her cons. One might claim that Bergman, with the very conceit and conception for this film, has pulled the greatest sleight of hand, in reference to the American title, and that is in convincing critics that this film neatly follows a pattern of depressing anti-religionism that other films in his canon do. But, a closer look shows this is all illusion, just as a closer look at Vogler, by the other characters, shows that he is just an illusionist. Nowhere is this better demonstrated but in his attic-bound assault on Vergerus's beliefs which, as the doctor correctly notes, proved nothing except that he is as susceptible to a momentary fear of death as any other mortal being.

That said, *The Magician* is not one of Bergman's deeper, nor more profound films, but, as someone willing to state that he does not 'like' most of Bergman's canon- even while admitting the greatness of a goodly number of his films, I can equally state that this is the most enjoyable of the films I've watched from the master. It plays out like an extended episode of the classic *The Twilight Zone* television series, with an appropriately ironic 'twist ending.' But, while not a great film, it is an excellent film, and sure to drive conversations long afterwards. Let's see….53 years and counting….not bad at all.

Film Review of *Reprise*
Copyright © by Dan Schneider, 2012

Sometimes one can watch a film and appreciate aspects of it, but see the totality and shrug. Such was the case when I watched Norwegian film director Joachim Trier's 2006 debut film *Reprise*. In a sense, it married the faux depth of European '70s cinema (aka Eurotrash) with modern Hollywood technical effects over substance to present a trite tale of two wannabe writers (replete with all the clichés of artsy types- from depression and sexual fetishism to suicide attempts and banal inquiries into the meaninglessness of existence) and their possibly faux reality of lives as famous writers. I say possibly and faux because the snarky '*what if?*' way the narrative of the film presents itself leaves open the possibility that the bulk of the film is a mere fantasy.

The film follows the lives of two 23 year old Upper Class Oslo writer pals, Erik (Espen Klouman Hoiner) and Phillip (Anders Danielsen Lie), who take two trajectories to becoming 'published' authors. Now, granted, I am an American, but something tells me that the ease with which these two Nordic slackers get published is all part of the fantasy element of the film (which is also dependent upon the fact that the audience never gets to see, hear, nor read even a sentence of the two young men's art, to determine its worth on its own right). Philip hits it big first, gets overnight fame (which seems to be the reason both men write- as they seem to be latterday wannabe Beatniks, not to create art, nor have an effect on others), gets depressed, has a doomed love affair, attempts suicide, gets institutionalized, released, and then gets writer's block. Erik is rejected, at first, then gets published, obsesses on a fictive Norwegian version of J.D. Salinger- rather predictably called Sten Egil Dahl (aka *Stendahl*- to contrast the older writer's 'realistic life' with their 'fantastical ones'), then goes abroad, becomes more famous, and reunites with Philip and his slacker buddies, who are a Nordic version of limp wristed wannabe skinheads.

The constant shaky camera movement, the breaks of 4th and 5th walls, the narrative abruptions, super-slick and quick edits, and what not, are all designed to mimic the worst in Hollywood style, but aim to enhance this with a supposed European depth. The problem is that there is not depth, and, in this sense, this film is clearly reminiscent- at least stylistically, of Jean-Luc Godard's massively overrated 1959 film, <u>Breathless</u>, and, indeed, most of this film's positive reviews, like those of *Breathless*, focus on the film's supposed aims, and how it impacted Norwegian film, not on the artistic nor narrative merits of the film. It may well be that *Reprise* was influential. But, so what? It's still a mediocre film, with mediocre acting (Lie is especially listless and unimpressive), bad scoring by Ola Fløttum and Knut Schreiner (with a punk rock themed soundtrack), mediocre cinematography by Jakob Ihre, and a mediocre script (written by Eskil Vogt and Trier). It's certainly not a bad film, and there are a few good moments of potential, and talent (Viktoria Winge, as Kari, Phillip's girlfriend, and this film's Jean Seberg, carries the scenes she's in), that show that this Trier has greater filmic talent than the more famous Lars Von Trier, but, unless that evinces itself in later films, again, so what?

The film ends on a STOP, but never is the viewer swept up enough in the tale of the two wannabes to care to go on, much less to care if what they have spent the prior 110 minutes watching was 'real' or 'fantasy'? I could go on , at length why the film fails to engender viewer care, but film critic Roger Ebert summed it up perfectly <u>in his review</u>:

> The big problem with the movie is our difficulty in working up much real interest in the characters. They're not compelling. Even when Phillip becomes so obsessed with Kari that he has to be accommodated in a mental institution, and even after (back on the streets) he takes her to Paris on the exact anniversary of

their first trip there, it's impossible to see him as passionate. His emotions never seem to be at full volume.

The high point, passion-wise, comes during their Paris trip. His mother has confiscated his photos of Kari, fearing they will trigger a relapse. So in Paris he poses her to take them again, Kari even helpfully hitching up her skirt to more closely match the original. They visit the same cafe (I think). Then they check into the same hotel and make love in (one assumes) much the same way.

The movie finds it necessary to do something I'm growing weary of: It depicts their lovemaking at greater length than depth. They're seen in profile, in dim lighting, with a soundtrack that reminded me of the Hondells "Little Honda" ("First gear, it's all right. Second gear, hold on tight"). After their breathing reaches overdrive, they disengage, and she soon enough says, "You don't still love me."

That word "love" is such a troublemaker. For characters like those in the movie, it represents an attainment like feeling patriotic or missing your dog. It's a state not consuming, not transcendent but obligatory.

What Ebert is getting at is that the film's pretense is that it makes much of its characters' pretense. To use the old cliché, Erik and Phillip are too busy trying to become writers that they have no idea how to be writers, and, worse, how to be normal people- at least as normal as an artist with talent can be. Finally, the film's gimmickry, from an unironic wannabe ironic omniscient narrator who pauses and rewinds scenes of action, to Erik's novel's title (*Prosopopoeia*) to Phillip's childish and foolish countdowns while closing his eyes, are simply too much to make this film anything more than a work that shows potential, talent, but no skill to martial the first two attributes.

In short, *Reprise* is a dumbed down, Americanized foreign film (in Norwegian, with borderless white English subtitles) that is earnest only in its efforts to be 'cool,' but, midway through, you know exactly how it will end, and it does nothing to prove you wrong. But, even removing those first two qualities, would still leave it an anomic mediocrity. You can exasperate now.

Film Review Of *Oslo, August 31st*
Copyright © by Dan Schneider, 2013

The 2011 sophomore feature film by Norwegian director Joachim Trier, *Oslo, August 31st*, is not a great film, but arguably a near great one, and a significantly better film than his debut work, 2006's *Reprise*. It stars Anders Danielson Lie, one of the two stars of that first film, as Anders, a drug addict out on a one day leave from his rehab program. The film chronologically starts on the morning of August 30th and ends the morning of August 31st. Structurally, it follows the lead of such classic films as Michelangelo Antonioni's *La Notte*, which followed the single night peregrinations of a couple that had fallen out of love, but it also follows the picaresque design of Federico Fellini's *La Dolce Vita*, wherein an anomic male protagonist's life of emptiness is displayed in a series of seven major vignettes that end at dawn. Trier's film never reaches the heights of those two films, because it is not a technically nor narratively bold enough film, but its unrelenting glare at the loneliness and depravity of its central character evokes the best of Ingmar Bergman's canon.

The 92 minute film opens with a montage sequence of people speaking their memories of Oslo, but we have no idea what they mean to the film, nor who the voices belong to. Then we meet Anders, a spoilt rich kid, now aged 34, who became an addict and dealer, waking up in the bed of a woman we have no idea the nature of. He leaves her, wanders through a forest, and attempts to drown himself in a lake, halfheartedly. By surviving, the film lets us know that, by its end, the character will end up relapsing, and, in terms of the screenplay, this is its biggest flaw, for we see the end coming almost right away from its start. Fortunately, the film is not about its trajectory, however predictable, but its glances to the sides of Anders' life, as his day ascends and descends to the ground.

Ostensibly, he gets a day pass from the rehab center he has been in for six years, to go on a job interview at a magazine. Before he goes to the interview, almost 30 minutes of the film is spent on his visit to an old friend of his, named Thomas (Hans Olav Brenner), who is married with kids. While we certainly gain insights into Anders' past, we also learn almost as much about Thomas- an Academic in a sexless and likely loveless union, and we sense that these men are people who were once close, but have nothing left in common. Anders' sneering at Thomas's bourgeois life is matched by Thomas's utter indifference to what is really wrong with Anders. Thomas's wife even calls him on the fact that generic platitudes show he is not really listening to his friend. The two men then leave his apartment and wander the town, where their conversation gets real and fascinating.

Anders decides to head for the interview, but, after a bit of evasiveness, comes clean that he has been in rehab, and, despite the sympathetic approach of the interviewer, kyboshes his own chances, with a critique of the magazine that is likely true, but deemed uppity by the interviewer. Throughout the film, Anders leaves messages on his ex-girlfriend Iselin's cell phone voicemail. She has moved to New York City and is clearly avoiding him. He seeks to reconcile, ostensibly, but really he hopes she will give him a way out of all the bad memories Oslo embodies. At a café he eavesdrops on conversations, then sees a blond woman pas by outside, and he imagines elements from her day, and we are left wondering if he believes this is Iselin or just random thoughts about an attractive woman. After the interview, Anders meets up at a party with another old girlfriend, and kisses her, after she details her anomic existence. He then leaves, after stealing some of her guest's money, goes to a dealer, buys either cocaine of heroin, goes to a bar, meets an old acquaintance, and a nubile college girl. They spend the night partying, and end up at a public swimming pool at dawn. Anders then leaves them, heads to his parents hone, which is on the market to help pay for his rehab. He plays a piano briefly, then shoots up, as the film ends and we see scenes of Oslo, quite reminiscent of the ending of Yasujiro Ozu's *Tokyo Story*.

Anders is alone. And, in this manner, *Oslo, August 31st* resembles Steve McQueen's *Shame*, save that McQueen's film is undeniably a great film. Both films' leads wander through their lives, afraid and/or unable to connect with each other. Both have addictions-drugs and sex, but both are alone, and their loneliness is what ails and propels them. Anders, however, seems the more likely of the two lonely characters to never recover. There are people from his past that he meets that distance themselves, newcomers that welcome, but only shallowly, and his family is AWOL. His parents are in Nice for a vacation, while his sister sends her lesbian lover (Tone Beate Mostrum) to tell him she needs time to deal with his impending release from rehab. Former friends at the ex-girlfriend's party make him the butt of a not too funny anecdote that he shrugs off, but which clearly stings, and then he tries to dickwave to a former lover of Iselin's, only to have the man put him in his place at a bar.

The screenplay, by Trier and Eskil Vogt, adapted from a 1931 novel, *Le Feu Follet*, by Pierre Drieu La Rochelle, which was also adapted by French filmmaker Louis Malle into 1963's *The Fire Within*, is a good one. But, it could have been great had there been a greater emphasis on the visual aspects of the film. Most modern films, especially from America, fail because the screenplays all give way to the visual razzle dazzle. In this case, a bit of Fellinian or Antonionian visual appeal could have added some devastatingly poetic moments to the film. Instead, the hand held camera's wobbliness comes off as rather dull and uninteresting to watch. Whether this flaw can be pinned on the director alone, or the cinematographer, Jakob Ihre, as well, is known only by them. The film's coring is apropos for the mood of the film, and this rates a recognition for Ola Flottum, who also allows the viewer to eavesdrop on conversations Anders overhears at assorted places in his wander. The all white subtitles are not the easiest to read, but, as the film is hot in color, and the dialogue is sparse, it is not a great disadvantage.

The film won many awards at film festivals, and is a positive sign that 21st century filmmaking has hope for the future, for Trier is just a notch or two below a new master filmmaker like Great Britain's Steve McQueen, yet could get to those heights if he continues his filmic development in the trajectory set by these first two films. Hopefully, *Oslo, August 31st* is not the high point in Trier's career.

Film Review Of *Pulp*
Copyright © by Dan Schneider, 2013

In 1971, director Mike Hodges and actor Michael Caine had a hit in the action thriller *Get Carter*. The following year they tried to do a comedic follow up to that film called *Pulp*, in which Caine played a mediocre pulp fiction crime novelist, Mickey King (who writes novels like *My Gun Is Long*, under the pseudonym Guy Strange), who, on holiday in Malta, gets involved with as former film star, Preston Gilbert (Mickey Rooney), who lures him into a web of murder and intrigue that lacks only one thing: intrigue. The problem is that the film is not well written, not well acted (Rooney is his usually atrocious self), and not really funny- especially bad is the forced narration that Caine's character speaks over the most rote action. Things get so bad that, in the worst way possible, Caine's voiceover either repeats an action we just saw onscreen, or anticipate sit, thus rendering the very point of a voiceover (the condensation of unnecessary action to get to dramatic 'meat') moot.

The joke of the film is that Gilbert was a B film star, who played gangsters, and associated with real world gangsters, back in the day. He is served by a valet named Ben Dinuccio (Lionel Stander), who approaches King with a large sum of money to ghost write the memoirs of Gilbert. Along the way to even meeting Gilbert, a homosexual and transvestite hitman named Miller (Al Lettieri) is killed in a hotel room meant to be taken by King, and a pseudo-romance emerges between King and one of Gilbert's female relatives. None of this is in the least bit interesting, nor are Rooney's onscreen tics and neuroses. When an assassin actually kills Gilbert, at an outdoor restraint, the guests think it's another of his elaborate gags. It's not.

King then quickly solves the so-called 'mystery,' which is just that King and some other partiers, years ago, got drunk and had sex with a girl, who died, mid-penetration, and the others decided to bury the body. When one of the other men heard Gilbert was penning his memoirs, he hired Miller, the hitman, to kill both Gilbert and King. But, since Miller was killed off earlier, who is the assassin on the loose?

Simple. It's Miller, who faked his death. This is easily seen, as, earlier in the film, no one even realizes Miller supposedly 'died.' But, through it all, one emotion overrides, and that is apathy. Simply put, a viewer simply feels nothing for any of these characters. They are so apathetically realized that they don't even rise to the level of stereotypes. All of this can be pinned on the bad screenplay by Hodges. The anomic cinematography, by Ousama Rawi, does not help matters. George Martin's scoring is also non-noteworthy, and often non-existent, in a negative sense. At times, the whole film feels like it was filmed by a bunch of college kids on spring break. About the only positive thing one can say about this film is that it only runs about 95 minutes in length.

Yet, oddly, it's not a film that is even bad enough to be memorable, therefore it doesn't even grate on one's mind. It's just utterly forgettable. And yes, there are odd little details that I could go into, but, I simply am not moved to do so. The film never even rewards its viewers for recognizing its details, so they become superfluous.

Regardless, *Pulp* is inoffensive, at least, in its sterile badness. It's not going to move you, in either direction, so, at least consider your bowels safe, for what it's worth.

Film Review Of *Peeping Tom*
Copyright © by Dan Schneider, 2011

One of the classes of film that a cinephile encounters is the film that is neither the masterpiece its champions proclaim, nor the dreck its detractors insist. A film that fits neatly into that category is Michael Powell's 1960 color film on a bizarre fetishist and serial killer, called *Peeping Tom*. To read about the 101 minute long film, one would think that it was as good or interesting a film as Albert Hitchcock's *Psycho*- a black and white film released the same year, and arguably, along with *The Birds*, Hitchcock's best. But, *Peeping Tom* is not in a league with *Psycho*, even if it does have moments, for, in reality, it's simply not a film that is scary in the least. In fact, the Hitchcock film it can most be compared to is 1972's *Frenzy*.

The film is, like most of Hitchcock's films, drenched in now long outdated Freudianism, but there is something to be said for the screenplay's boldness, in presenting the situation of a man, Mark Lewis (Karlheinz Boehm), tormented by a dead genius father (the reverse of *Psycho*'s dead mother fixation), who filmed and recorded his son's every move and utterance, ostensibly for scientific research, yet who succeeds in driving his son crazy. Also, Mark's desire to kill whatever is frightened of him does take on an oddly believable texture when he refuses to look at the girl who rents a room in his home, Helen Stephens (Anna Massey). Her mother (Maxine Audley), although blind, suspects Mark of deviance, if not murder, and the best scene in the film is a de facto cat and mouse game in Mark's secret film room, where he masturbates over the snuff films he creates, where Anna's mother warns him of a need to confess. She states, to him, 'I visit this room every night. The blind always visit the rooms they live under. What am I seeing, Mark?' But, more often than not the film's few strengths are undone by its weaknesses- most notably, stiff and ineffective acting.

The film opens following a prostitute being filmed in her last death throes, pursued by Mark and his camera with a deadly tripod, as well as a mirror attached, which allows the viewer to experience ea bit of the main character's voyeurism, but the whole situation is absurdly contrived, for, carrying his lumbering instrument of death, this killer would be absurdly easy to avoid, then kick the ass of, considering how fey mark really is. *Psycho*, in this way, with the knife wielding Norman Bates, who attacks his victims while they are unawares, is far more realistic. Mark's murders are contrived and, frankly, silly. The lamest one is the killing of Powell's star of *The Red Shoes*, Moira Shearer, who plays Vivian, an extra on the film, *The Walls Are Closing In*, that Mark is working on as a cameraman (technically, a focus puller), for he lures her to a death that even a retard, much less a healthy and athletic woman, could avoid. The actual best part of that murder- one of three Mark commits in the film, comes when he later films the police detectives gathering evidence at the crime scene. His ending suicide, once he's found out, is equally melodramatic and silly, and the way he's found out is simply stupid, as is the predictable way Helen, who is falling for the shy and fey cameraman from a local film studio, stumbles across his snuff films. Yet, the film is rumored to have sunk Michael Powell's career as a serious filmmaker.

The film, shown in a full screen, 1.35:1 aspect ratio, was directed by Powell, sand his longtime partner Emeric Pressburger, and the screenplay was written by Leo Marks. The basic problem with the script is the utter banality of its premise, for, not only is Mark an aspiring filmmaker, but he shoots porno for a local news vendor, and, no surprise, ends up murdering one of his subjects. On the other hand, the film does have good moments, such as an earlier scene, photographing girls, where Mark gets fascinated by a physically deformed girl's eyes. Unfortunately, these more realistic moments are buried under an avalanche of the gauche, predictable, and trite. The film's soundtrack, likely its greatest asset, was created by Brian Easdale, who did such a magnificent job on *The Red Shoes*. The cinematography, by Otto Heller, is good, but nothing spectacular. Filmed mostly on studio lots, the film has both a fake and cheap feel to it, even though it was not shot as low budget as *Psycho* was.

Despite all the critical cribbing, and misinterpretations of the film's themes and excellence, perhaps the most observant criticism of the film came from the New York Times' critic, Vincent Canby, who wrote:

> When Michael Powell's "Peeping Tom" was originally released in England, in 1960, the critics rose up like a bunch of furious Reverend Davidsons to condemn it on moral grounds. "It stinks," one critic wrote. Another thought it should be flushed down the sewer, and a third dismissed it haughtily as "perverted nonsense." There is nothing angrier than a critic when he can be safely outraged.

He then made these cogent remarks:

> "Peeping Tom's" rediscovery, I fear, tells us more about fads in film criticism than it does about art. Only someone madly obsessed with being the first to hail a new auteur, which is always a nice way of calling attention to oneself, could spend the time needed to find genius in the erratic works of Mr. Powell — "One of Our Aircraft Is Missing," "The Life and Death of Colonel Blimp," "The Red Shoes," "Tales of Hoffman" and so on, all directed with Emeric Pressberger, and "Peeping Tom," which he directed alone….What seems to fascinate "Peeping Tom's" new supporters is Mr. Powell's appreciation of the idea that the act of photographing something can be an act of aggression, of violation….This fascination dates back to the movie-mad 60's, when movies became Art, film schools began to flourish, and the taking of moving pictures seemed to offer an easy way to self-expression and possibly celebrity….I am, perhaps, somewhat prejudiced. As interested as I am in films, the properties of the movie camera are not, for me, a subject of endless fascination. The movie camera is not magical. It's a tool, like a typewriter….I find it difficult to become morally outraged by "Peeping Tom" and even more difficult to see this movie as anything more than an excruciatingly schematic, very solemn melodrama, quite badly acted by everyone.

All in all, Canby nails the film better than any of the critics who loathe or adore the film, and is especially right about Boehm's performance, which seems to be channeling Peter Lorre's sniveling characters on a bad day, when it's not merely being wooden and dull. Yet, there are the good parts, and the potentially good parts, which could have led to Peeping Tom being erotic, scary, and complex. Unfortunately, the film is just a well wrought mediocrity. Where *Psycho* stands, half a century on, as still a near great film, and one of Hitchcock's best works, *Peeping Tom*'s legacy is that of a film that is difficult to understand why it so outraged, upon its release, and why it so fascinates so many today, given its limited successes and manifest failures. To me it's just- *<yawn>*

Film Review Of *Black Narcissus*
Copyright © by Dan Schneider, 2012

   Directors Michael Powell and Emeric Pressburger's 1947 film, *Black Narcissus*, has
been called many things- from a condescending work in support of imperialism (it
actually damns the condescenders) to the greatest Technicolor film ever made (an
arguable proposition), but in my watching of it, its true nature came forth: it is one of the
best tracts against religion, specifically, and conformism, generally, ever made, and,
while it served as a visual template for Alfred Hitchcock's far inferior *Vertigo*, it more
accurately served as a bridge between old time Hollywood horror films, and those of
German Expressionism, and the more existential horror films of the 1960s, from the
Hammer films, to Italian horror, to the apex of the genre, in *Night Of The Living Dead*.
   Yes, most critics label this 100 minute long film a melodrama, or a meditation on faith,
but make no mistake, from the earliest scenes of the film, where lead actress Deborah
Kerr, as Sister Clodagh, gets assigned as the Sister Superior to a high Himalayan outpost,
donated to the nuns' order by an Indian general, by the Mother Superior of her then
current convent, presumably in Calcutta, the film is awash in evil, as the Mother Superior
(Nancy Roberts) seemingly picks the nuns who will work with Clodagh out of some
sadistic need to pick the weakest and most vulnerable women to be tested. The very look
of sadism resides in the Mother Superior's mien, as she seems to know that she is
dooming them in a high mountain hell, not unlike the fate that awaits Jack Torrance and
his clan in Stanley Kubrick's *The Shining*. Later in the film, there is a justifiably famous
scene where Sister Ruth (Kathleen Byron) smiles menacingly at Sister Clodagh, not
unlike the female vampire in Carl-Theodor Dreyer's *Vampyr*, and it shows plainly that
she's on a different plane of reality, but most people forget the twisted sneer of hate that
dominates the Mother Superior's mien early on, for it is even more chilling, as she knows
what her religion and conformity have cost her, and she simply cannot wait to make her
underlings suffer as much for their own personal Christs.
   After assigning five nuns to their own private hells, the Mother Superior is never seen
again, and the nuns arrive at their retreat, the Palace Of Mopu, where a former Raj held
his courtesans, ensconced on a cliffside, 8000 feet up. There, they encounter the natives,
whom they often belittle as if children, and set about to launch their nunnery, mission,
health clinic, and school for children, all at the behest of the current 'General' (Esmond
Knight) of the region. The General's British agent, or go between, is Mr. Dean (David
Farrar), a handsome, rugged 'man of adventure' who would be the star of most films set
in such an exotic locale, but who is a definite third fiddle in this film, behind Sisters
Clodagh and Ruth, who both clearly desire him sexually. He, however, as an irreligiot,
has no interest in either of them, although the film does hint that he has his way with
many of the local women, including a beautiful seventeen year old wanton native girl
named Kanchi (Jean Simmons), who ends up seducing and running away with the
General's son, the Young General (Sabu), who also studies at the convent. Dean has little
patience and truck with the sisters, and says that their mission won't even make it to the
next rainy season. The sexual tension between him and Clodagh is palpable- especially
for a 1940s film, and one can see that this film would never have been made in
Hollywood.
   Although the Clodagh-Ruth wannabe triangle with Dean is the center of the surface
drama, there are other subplots that hint at how repression and conformity destroy lives.
Sister Honey (Jenny Laird) is a weak willed girl who doubts herself constantly, Sister
Briony (Judith Furse) is a butch woman whose dubious medical skills result in the death
of a native child, which forms the central climax of the film. Before this death, which

Sister Honey foolishly tries to assist on, after Briony gives up, the nuns seem to be succeeding in their mission. After it, the sisters are doomed. Even Sister Philippa (Flora Robson), the oldest of the nuns, suffers depression, deliberately plants flowers instead of vegetables, for she searches for spiritual- not bodily, nourishment, and wants to be transferred, so that he career will be stained, for the new mission reminds her of feelings she had long thought she'd suppressed; a condition which inflicts Clodagh even more, as memories of a failed teen romance, in her native Ireland, haunt her, which leads to her imbuing old sexual feelings for her lost beau onto Dean. These flashbacks to her lost love were banned from the film for decades, as they suggested that Clodagh was not as virtuously imperious in her 'wild youth.' Perhaps the most odd, yet humorous, character in the film (other than the unmoving mute local holy man) is a local woman who takes care of the palace, called Angu Ayah (May Hallatt). She's clearly insane, sadistic, and openly contemptuous of the nuns- even more so than Dean.

Yet, the main character of the film is not any of the human ones; it's as I stated: religion, specifically, and conformity, generally; twin evils that are given a Gothic horror treatment by film's end. And Michael Powell was absolutely correct when he suggested the film was his most erotic: there is nary a scene in cinema history that is as personally orgasmic to a character as the seen where Sister Ruth dashes her all white habit, wears a sexy, dress, and then applies lipstick in front of Clodagh. Technically, the film is a marvel, with no real scenes of the Himalayas used- it was all done with matte shots, and this is that rare film that benefits from the artificiality of the backgrounds, for it heightens the dream aspects of the film, as well as the Expressionistic horror that comes to an estrogenic boil when Ruth tries to push Clodagh off the bell ringing station (interesting trivia- Kerr was the Powell's ex-lover, and Byron his then current one), at cliff's edge, that conveniently lacks any guard rail; a plot point that is one of the few missteps in the screenplay, for, from the moment I first saw that, I knew someone was going to plummet to their death. Nonetheless, Byron's performance as Sister Ruth dominates the last half hour of the film, and the combination of the rich, saturated colors, the deep, long shadows, and the mania of Ruth makes the film a thriller, at its end.

Yet, there are a number of films that this one holds truck with- some I've already mentioned, but one which will surprise many, and that is George Stevens' cowboy classic, _Shane_. Both films take classical tropes that could easily have become clichéd in lesser works, but which embody the very things the clichés merely erect as husks. In _Shane_, scenes and characters and motifs are ennobled and made greater by a number of means, but most specifically the taking of all these things and casting them through the prism of a young boy's hero worship. In _Black Narcissus_, scenes and characters and motifs are twisted through the cynical balancing of Dean's nihilism and Ruth's deadly loneliness. Both show the folly of the nuns' plights, which becomes the spiritual equivalent of the material folly suffered by the soldiers in the neglected great film, _The Desert Of The Tartars_, for they help turn what could have been yet another stuffy, exotic 1940s film into a plangent and cogent meditation on evil- right or wrong- via psychotic nuns. That is a trick worth admiring, if nothing else. But there is much more.

Technically, the film was at the forefront of its art, at the time, and won well earned Academy Awards for Best Art Direction and Best Cinematograph, and cinematographer, Jack Cardiff's handiwork (and Vermeerian use of light) threads through this film like few pre-New Wave cinematographers' work do. Powell and Pressburger's screenplay, based on Rumer Godden's novel of the same name really does everything right, including the changes that are detailed in many articles online, for they all work to enhance the film, apart from the book. The film's score, by Brian Easdale, is also well suited for the film, and it is the type of score that is often overlooked, for it is not immediately 'memorable,' in the way that of *2001: A Space Odyssey*'s or *The Good, The Bad And The Ugly*'s are, but it blends in seamlessly with the emotional content of the screenplay and the tenor set by the actors and directors. In this way, the score is sort of like the scent of the once mentioned flower the film takes its title from- it works subliminally, and this is another reason for this film's greatness, for, unlike the excellent, but not great, film Powell and Pressburger made, right after this one, *The Red Shoes*, this film never hammers one over the head with what it is doing. Yes, it's fine with the misassumptions of bad critics and viewers, but this film *is* going to deal its message to you, by guile or syringe, if not dint nor hammer. *Black Narcissus* is about loneliness and loss, and, in the end, arguably about the loss of loneliness, and acceptance, for, by film's end, even though the nuns leave (yes, before the rains come), defeated by the thing that is India, and the man that is Dean, they all know what they want, and that is not what they had- that thing all religions and sorts of conformity necessarily kill, for they have gained *themselves*.

Film Review Of *The Red Shoes*
Copyright © by Dan Schneider, 2011

The 1948 film, *The Red Shoes*, directed by Michael Powell and Emeric Pressburger, is often called the greatest ballet film ever, and that may well be so, for it is an excellent film, clocking in at 93 minutes in length. But the thing that stands out about it, in the non-diegetic realm, is how critically abysmal most critics have been in regard to it, and that is because they cannot realize that, despite its being shot in Technicolor, and featuring a slight romance, this British film is nothing like most Hollywood fare of the day, nor now, and, in fact, is one of the earliest cinematic attempts at portraying the effects of monomania, and its results: loneliness, grief, and regret, which misses out on greatness because of a few poor choices and being a bit too socially precocious for its own good.

It follows the rise and fall of an aristocratic wannabe ballerina, Victoria 'Vicky' Page (Moira Shearer) who rises in the ballet company of an autocratic but arts-obsessed owner of the company: Boris Lermontov (Anton Walbrook), and Lermontov's obsession with Vicky is the thing most critics flail on. He is often posited as gay, or being 'in love' with Vicky, and domineering, to possess her and take her away from the talented young composer, Julian Craster (Marius Goring), Lermontov has engaged, and is similarly rising in the company, and who has fallen in love with Vicky. But this is nonsense, as not a single scene, glance between Walbrook and Shearer, nor an uttered word, gives any sense that there is a love felt by Lermontov, save for a deep, almost desperate love for art (witness how Lermontov retains the rights to the ballet of *The Red Shoes* and Julian's score, and refuses to produce it again or let anyone else produce it)- and art is the one thing that inspires a passion in some humans that almost all critics cannot grasp, as they are not creative artists themselves. Critic Roger Ebert even dismissively relegates Lermontov, in this manner: '*the impresario defies analysis. In his dark eyes we read a fierce resentment.*' After Lermontov convinces Vicky to leave her lover, he as much says so, when Julian comes to fetch her, leaving the opening night of his own opera, he says: 'You're jealous of her.' Lermontov says, defiantly, 'Yes, I am. But in a way you'll never understand.' And it is clear that, although Julian is a creator of art, he does not understand it to the depths that an aficionado- a soul committed to art alone, can. And this is shown even earlier in the film, when Lermontov rails at a former ballerina's abandonment of her career when she falls in love; so, clearly, there is no sexual jealousy over Vicky involved; merely Lermontov's belief that love is a distraction great art should do without.

In fact, this is a *film* in love with the arts, even as it shows the cruel and brute nature of it, in scenes that are so raw and real it is almost shocking that they were filmed only a few years after World War Two, because, most British cinema was far too staid, in that era, to show such realism, and, any greatness the film contains comes not from the dull, unconvincing romance between Vicky and Julian, but in the unrelenting portrait of the monomania of Lermontov, who, in a sense, chases and artistically destroys Vicky in an Ahabian pursuit. The film's denouement, where, as in the original fairy tale, by Hans Christian Andersen, the red shoes have a life of their own, seems to play out in a similar fashion here, but, this makes the ending rather childish and silly, and is a great comedown after the brilliant moments that the film earlier proposes. Notably, many critics posit things in the film that simply are not so, from Julian's and Vicky's relationship, to Lermontov's motives, and even till the end of the film where, amazingly, after a fall and seemingly being run over by a train, Vicky survives.... yet most critics, as in the later *Au Hasard Balthazar*, claim she has died. Yet, there is no evidence for this. Surely she would have died instantly, from the height she falls, and from being run over dead on; yet she asks Julian to remove the shoes. Granted, whether or not she dies is irrelevant for the childish ending, for it detracts from the film no matter; the important point is that the main subject of the film is Lermontov and his love of art- a things so pure that he performs The Red Shoes without Vicky, but with a spotlight shining where she would have.

The film is brilliantly restored, and Technicolor never looked so good. The surrealism shown in the first performance of *The Red Shoes* is the bravura highlight of the film, but the scenes showing the cattiness of the audition process also shines. The screenplay, by Powell, Pressburger, and Keith Winter, shines, and the film has many excellent moment, but, even if the film had lacked the disappointing ending, it still misses out on greatness because of a number of superfluous and predictably banal scenes involving other members of the Lermontov ballet company. And, while Shearer and Goring's romance is contrived, they do make a go at the whole 'in love' thing, even if little of their wooing is shown, and the pair seem to lack any chemistry. But the film belongs to Walbrook's Lermontov. Lermontov does not steal every scene he's in; he dominates every scene. Jack Cardiff's cinematography is solid, but the film shines in its surreal special effects scene in the first performance of *The Red Shoes*. Brian Easdale's musical score is sparkling and memorable.

That the film died at the box office is a testament to the fact that, even in the 'Golden Age' of one form of art or another, there is always a vein of Philistinism afoot. Yet, perhaps the worst review of the film out there, is from a critic named Carter B. Horsley. It starts off with this sentence:

> Although it has been widely acclaimed as the greatest "dance" film in history, *The Red Shoes* is the greatest film in history, period.

Let's see: *2001: A Space Odyssey*, *La Dolce Vita*, *Blowup*, *Taxi Driver*….Nope, *The Red Shoes* doesn't measure up. A good film, but not great.

But, then it goes almost wholly into critical cribbing mode, and goes with a fallacy:

> Two men are in love with the same woman. One is powerful and the other creative. One offers her the opportunity to fulfill herself as a great artist. The other as a woman.
>
> It's not an easy choice, actually, as this movie, more than any other, so dramatically shows.

After a few pages of blather, Horsley utterly shows his simpleminded bias, enduing the review this way:

> This is the best film of all time, because it is a great love story, a great moral story, because of Shearer's incandescence and because no other film has dared to better another art form at its own game and won as convincingly.

In other words, the critic loves childish romances, moralizing, Shearer is hot, and he thinks he knows what the film is about, but clearly doesn't. The problem, of course, is that Horsley is hardly a lone nutjob out there. Most critics, while not as stultifyingly dumb, are just as clueless.

What *The Red Shoes* does, via the power of Lermontov's vision, is show how utterly important art can and should be to people who are not even creative themselves. Recall, that Lermontov, while a mere businessman, understands this power far deeper than a presumably talented artist like Julian. The film also argues, almost persuasively, that this import should extend to the interpretive arts, as dancing, as well as the creative arts, for this is precisely the crux of what is at the center of the Lermontov, Vicky, and Julian non-sexual triangle. *The Red Shoes* would have been a great film, had its lens been focused far more on Lermontov- who he is, what drives him, and why he cannot refrain from the destructive impulses his compulsion achieves, but 1948 was still too early for the British cinematic chrysalis to grasp the ideas that even one of its best films was making, and this is what leads to the film's ultimate failure at greatness. Later films, like *Taxi Driver* (whose director, Martin Scorsese, has long cited *The Red* Shoes as a seminal film in his understanding of cinema) would run with the ideas that this film presents, that compulsions- even if derived from positive virtues (like a love of art) are almost always destructive- be it of the self, or others, but, this film makes a brave go at such, in an innocent time. However, no amount of courage can make up for what the film lacks, thus it is merely an excellent film- one of the great *could've beens*, instead of the *wases*. There are worse fates, ladies and gentlemen. Good night.

Film Review Of *Breaker Morant*
Copyright © by Dan Schneider, 2013

Such is the power of Stanley Kubrick's great 1957 film, _Paths Of Glory_, that its greatness makes all other films on the hypocrisy of military leaders look so-so in its wake. Such a notion graced my mind as I watched Bruce Beresford's 1980 film, *Breaker Morant*, which follows an eerily similar tale (both based on true stories) about three sacrificial military lambs, in its 107 minute running time. This Australian color film follows the court martial of Lt. Harry 'Breaker' Morant (Edward Woodward), and two of his underlings- Lts. George Witton (Lewis Fitz-Gerald) and Peter Handcock (Bryan Brown), in the Boer War, in turn of the 20th Century South Africa. They were members of the Colonial Bushveldt Carbineers.

They are charged with the murders of a Boer prisoner, six Boer guerillas, and a German pastor who was aiding and abetting the enemy. On the first two counts, the charges are bogus. The third one end sup being true, but, as it was during wartime, the three men are simply being set up for political reasons, as pawns to forestall a German entry into the war on the Boer side. The people who testify against them are all cravens who have their own reasons to lie, the court is a bunch of military political hacks, the superiors who know that the trio were just following the orders of Lord Kitchener (Alan Cassell) have all been transferred out of South Africa- a tactic Kitchener soon follows, and their token defense counsel is Major J. F. Thomas (Jack Thompson), an inheritance lawyer with just one day to prepare. Thompson gives perhaps the best performance in the film- even better than the more showoffy- yet still excellent, performance by Woodward, and one of the better portrayals of a lawyer in film history, with one of the better summations:

> Now, I don't ask for proclamations condoning distasteful methods of war, but I do say that we must take for granted that it does happen. Let's not give our officers hazy, vague instructions about what they may or may not do. Let's not reprimand them, on the one hand for hampering the column with prisoners, and at another time and another place, hold them up as murderers for obeying orders.
>
> The fact of the matter is that war changes men's natures. The barbarities of war are seldom committed by abnormal men. The tragedy of war is that these horrors are committed by normal men in abnormal situations, situations in which the ebb and flow of everyday life have departed and have been replaced by a constant round of fear, and anger, blood, and death. Soldiers at war are not to be judged by civilian rules, as the prosecution is attempting to do, even though they commit acts which, calmly viewed afterwards, could only be seen as unchristian and brutal. And if, in every war, particularly guerilla war, all the men who committed reprisals were to be charged and tried as murderers, court martials like this one would be in permanent session. Would they not?

In the end, Witton, a young man, is sentenced to death, but has his sentence commuted to life in prison by Kitchener, while the other two are found guilty and shot the next morning. In the film's epilogue, we learn that Witton, in 1907, wrote a book called *Scapegoats Of The Empire*, which, along with the stage play *Breaker Morant*, by Kenneth G. Ross, served as the basis for the film's screenplay. Morant, a minor poet, got his nickname for being a breaker of horses.

But, whereas, in *Paths Of Glory*, all three scapegoats are killed, and are innocent, in reality, it turns out that only Witton is possibly innocent. Morant and Handcock definitely murdered the preacher. The only question is whether it was justifiable since he was clearly in league with the enemy. Handcock even goes so far as to claim to have had sex with two married Boer women right after his killing of the preacher, to hide his guilt. And then angry Boers storm the British prison, in an attempt to free and kill the three prisoners, yet they save the day and fend off the enemy. Yet, even this does not get them, at least, a pardon, if not apology.

The screenplay, by Jonathan hardy, David Stevens, and Beresford, is good, but a bit dry, at times. Yes, it is a courtroom drama, but a bit more on the actual incidents would have sufficed. Also, going the tired flashback route is always the safe route. Donald McAlpine's cinematography is solid, but not spectacular. The bluish day for night shots are particularly ineffective. Shown in a 1.78:1 aspect ratio, the film's strengths are almost all derived from the actual history and the acting performances, not any cinematic techniques. This difference between Kubrick and Beresford, Paths Of Glory and Breaker Morant, shows how important the separate artistic techniques of film are in lifting film above total dependence on a screenplay.

Breaker Morant is a good film, often a very good film, but *Paths Of Glory* is great- one of the all time best films on war and its ugliness. *Breaker Morant*, in comparison, both filmically and rhetorically, looks and feels like a first draft in a similar key. Would that many of the gushing critics, both at its release, and in the decades since, gotten that note, then, perhaps, filmmakers would be more in tune with the vagaries of two of mankind's most important pursuits: war….and great art.

Film Review Of *Things You Can Tell Just By Looking At Her*
Copyright © by Dan Schneider, 2012

The 2000 film, *Things You Can Tell Just By Looking At Her*, which clocks in at 109 minutes in length, by Rodrigo Garcia, was his debut film, and not quite up to his great 2005 film *Nine Lives*, even though, within the earlier film, one can see the makings of greatness just coming to fruition.

The film is divided into five major stories, separated by title cards, and characters bounce in and out of each others' tales. It opens with a prelude: police detectives, in an unnamed city (presumably Los Angeles), find a dead woman in a motel room. The woman, a portly Latina (Elpidia Carillo), turns out to be an old high school classmate of lead detective Kathy Faber (Amy Brenneman). Her unknown reasons and fate set the template for the other tales. The first is *This Is Dr. Keener*, and follows the titular Elaine Keener (Glenn Close), a divorcee having an affair with a co-worker, as she takes care of her elderly mother. She gets a visit from a local psychic named Christine (Calista Flockhart), who delivers a glum, yet very vague, assessment of Keener's life, which the doctor takes to heart. The only positive in the tarot card reading is that Elaine is left with some hope, as she is told that a younger man will soon enter her life.

The second tale is *Fantasies About Rebecca*, which follows a self-destructive bank manager, Rebecca (Holly Hunter), who smokes, has an affair with a married black man, Robert (Gregory Hines), gets pregnant and has an abortion. The talk between the two, over the abortion is very realistic and nonchalant. Meanwhile, she has a one night stand with her assistant manager, Walter (Matt Craven), then blows him off, and has a few rather obvious and poorly sketched out scenes with a nasty homeless woman named Nancy (Penelope Allen). Up to this point, the film was doing everything right. The addition of the homeless savant is a too easy and trite trope in this tale. To make matters worse, the vignette ends, after Rebecca has the abortion, sees Nancy, and starts weeping uncontrollably. After such a mature and realistic approach to the abortion (including seeing Dr. Keener performing the abortion on her), to end with such a noxious PC cliché, is shameful and unrealistic screenwriting.

The third tale, *Someone for Rose*, is the weakest in the film, and follows a schoolteacher and children's author, Rose (Kathy Baker), who is a single mother with a bizarre fixation on her 15 year old son, Jay (Noah Fleiss). Across the street, a dwarf named Albert (Danny Woodburn) move sin and the two characters bizarrely flirt. The fourth tale is also relatively weak, as it follows Christine the psychic, from the first tale, in *Good Night Lilly, Good Night Christine*. Christine is a lesbian whose lover, Lilly (Valeria Golino), is dying. Not much occurs but severe handwringing. Again, there are some moments, but the PC attitude drags the whole tale down. The last tale, *Love Waits For Kathy*, is the best, and follows the detective, Kathy Faber, from the prelude, as she tries to connect the dots in her old classmate's death. She lives with her blind sister, Carol (Cameron Diaz), who goes out and sleeps with Walter, from the second tale, until both are disillusioned. Kathy ends up with no real answers to the mystery of the old classmate's suicide, but ends up going out with the coroner on the case.

The film also has an epilogue, wherein we see small moments from all the main characters, and the film ends with Dr. Keener at a bar, where she meets, and gets a light for her cigaret from Walter. The film is at its best when viewers see the connecting aspects of the film: such as Rose at the bank, doing business with Walter, Christine seeing the dead Latina in her dreams- for they were friends, Detective Faber asking for medical records from Albert the dwarf, who works at the hospital, and so on. This

52

unresolved realism is the film's strengths, whereas its weaknesses are in the delves into unrealistic plot points and Politically Correct nonsense.

The film was made for a theatrical release, and got it overseas, where it won some awards at film festivals- including Cannes, but opened on cable tv stateside, where Holly Hunter was nominated for an Emmy Award. Written by Garcia, it has some great moments and some not so good ones, which prevent it from any claims on greatness, the way *Nine Lives* does. The scoring, by Edward Shearmer, is solid, but the cinematography, by Emmanuel Lubezki, is marred by a number of scenes and vignettes with a dark filter on the top of the screen- a thing that seems to be endemic and intentional to the film, in both DVD and streaming versions- which I saw on Netflix.

Nonetheless, *Things You Can Tell Just By Looking At Her* is a good film, and one which contained seeds of greater things. I recommend it, especially in contrast with the mass of cinema that graces the airwaves these days.

Film Review Of *Shoeshine*
Copyright © by Dan Schneider, 2012

   Clocking in at 87 minutes long, Italian film director Vittorio De Sica's first major film
success, *Shoeshine* (*Sciuscià (Raggazzi)*), a 1946 black and white Neo-Realism classic, is
a good, solid film, but nowhere in a class with the director's later Neo-Realistic classics,
The Bicycle Thief and *Umberto D.*. The chief reason for this is that, despite its claims to
being Neo-Realism, in fact, the film is really far more in tune with the socially conscious
films coming out of Hollywood in the 1930s, during the Great Depression; especially
those put forth by the Warner Brothers film studio (think the Dead End Kids) for two
main rasons- 1) the film makes use of elaborate sets, not real settings, therefore it cannot
technically be Neo-Realism, and 2) it is pure melodrama. Of course, neither of these
reasons exclude the film from being good nor enjoyable. It is both of these things. But it
is not a great film, even if it points the way forward for De Sica, as an artist with
potential.
   The film follows two young Roman shoeshine boys, in the early post-War era of Italy,
Giuseppe (Rinaldo Smordoni) and Pasquale (Franco Interlenghi)- who is 2-3 years older
than Guiseppe. They dream of buying a horse so they can charge fees for riding, and
conscientiously save up almost enough money to do so. Then, one day, Giuseppe's older
brother, Attilio (Atiello Mele), hooks them up with a local con man- a fence who wants to
unload some stolen American blankets. The boys decide to sell them to another con- a
fortune teller (Maria Campi), who buys them. A few seconds later, Attilio, the con man,
and his pal, pretend they are cops, and pretend they will charge her with buying stolen
goods. They pretend to arrest the boys, then pay them off for the con. Now the boys have
enough to buy their horse. But, on the way home, that night, the fortune teller and some
real cops, nab them, and charge them with the theft of large sums of money from the
fortune teller, hoping the boys will rat out the older cons who set them up as the fall guys.
   The boys clam up and are arrested, then sent to a juvenile prison. Brief scenes of how
other boys are treated let the viewer know that nothing good awaits them in their
newfound predicament. Giuseppe and Pasquale are split up into different cells, and
eventually make friends with their four other cellmates. When Giuseppe gets a package
from his family, it has a note instructing him to keep quiet. He tells Pasquale and they
agree. The two boys are then interrogated, then threatened with beatings. Giuseppe is led
away, and back to his cell, but Pasquale is fooled into thinking he is being whipped, as
the cop beats a sandbag, and a rat fink kid, who is also an inmate, cries out as if he is
Giuseppe. To prevent his friend from being beaten, Pasquale cracks, and confesses all,
only to learn he was fooled shortly thereafter, when he sees Giuseppe is ok in his cell.
Pasquale does not admit he was tricked into ratting. Giuseppe finds out his brother was
arrested, and accuses Pasquale of being a traitor. His own cellmates egg him on into his
newfound hatred of his longtime friend. Giuseppe's cellmate, and leader of their cell,
Arcangeli (Bruno Ortenzi), sets Pasquale up, by planting a file in his bunk, then having
Giuseppe fink on Pasquale. This sets up tension in a shower scene (full of young male
nudity- a homosexual masturbatory heaven!), but the two friends try to reconcile. Seeing
his plan on the verge of failing, Arcangeli berates Giuseppe, picks a fight with Pasquale,
and gets his ass kicked.
   Later, in their cell, Arcangeli berates Giuseppe for wanting to forgive Pasquale, despite
knowing his friend was tricked into revealing the truth. Arcangeli then formulates a
prison break. Giuseppe gets a lawyer, paid for by his family, and this requires him to turn
on Pasquale, who is homeless and has both parents dead. Pasquale gets a public defender
who barely does anything. Giuseppe gets a year and a fine, while Pasquale pulls two and

a half years, and a larger fine. Back in prison, Giuseppe and his cellmates plan their escape during a film show. But, they are found out, and in the turmoil of their escape, one boy is trampled to death, and a fire and panic ensue. Plotting revenge, or just being angry that Giuseppe escaped without him, Pasquale tells the warden he knows where Giuseppe went, then leads them to the stable where the horse they bought was kept. The authorities find the stable master beaten and he tells the cops that Arcangeli and Giuseppe escaped on the horse. During all this, Pasquale makes his break, and catches up with the two boys on the horse, by a bridge over a creek. The cowardly Arcangeli flees, while Giuseppe is beaten by Pasquale, with his belt. Trying to avoid more pain, Giuseppe trips and falls off the bridge and onto the rocks below, and dies. Pasquale is overcome with grief, as the authorities arrive.

There is little more to tell, as one can presume Pasquale will be incarcerated for decades, for murder and escaping from the warden's men, but, as mentioned, thi sis in no way a Neo-Realistic film. Yes, its critique of Italian society, and juvenile justice, in that era, is deservedly harsh. It criminalized base survival, then issued punishment guaranteed to be worse than the so-called 'crimes.' But, it is pure melodrama, and rather predictable. Arcangeli, as example, is the typical coward, using younger kids to do his dirty work, then running, literally or figuratively, when things go wrong.

The none too subtly emotionally manipulative screenplay, written by Sergio Amidei, Adolfo Franci, Cesare Giulio Viola, and Cesare Zavattini, is solid, but not spectacular, and the film's score, by Alessandro Cicognini, is, in many ways, off the rack. The music never overbears, but neither does it inspire nor fulfill a moment. The cinematography, by Anchise Brizzi, and the editing by Niccolò Lazzari are also solid but not spectacular. But the film succeeds on the strength of its two male leads, Smordoni and Interlenghi, especially Interlenghi, who went on to a long career in film. Interlenghi gives a performance of depth, and for a then 15 year old, this is a rare thing. One almost sees what thoughts he is having via his gaze. Smordoni is not as good, but not nearly as bad as many critics have claimed.

I streamed the film on Netflix, and it is a solid print, shot in 1.33:1 aspect ratio, but the film's borderless white subtitles are difficult to read, as they are quite small. The American DVD for this film is released by The Criterion Collection, but this is likely not the same print, for the font and font size given are not matches with Criterion's usual. The film did win an Oscar for Best Foreign Film. While *Shoeshine* is not a great film, it is an important film in the Neo-Realist canon, and an enjoyable film, even if its flaws have perdured more persistently than its graces.

Film Review Of *Mafioso*
Copyright © by Dan Schneider, 2012

Italian film director Alberto Lattuada is a mostly forgotten figure in world and Italian cinema these days, best known for having given Federico Fellini his start in films by letting him co-direct *Variety Lights* in 1950. With an oeuvre that is hit and miss, one of his hits is 1962's black and white drama-comedy, *Mafioso*, which runs 105 minutes. The film stars Alberto Sordi, one of Italy's best comic and light dramatic actors, and his skills are put on ample display in this film, where he portrays Antonio (Nino) Badalamenti, a Sicilian boy made good in the big northern city of Milan, where he has a posh management job in an auto factory, as well as a beautiful blond wife, Marta (Norma Bengell), and two lovely young blond daughters, Cinzia (Cinzia Bruno) and Caterina (Katiusca Piretti). After years of putting off a vacation he decides to take fifteen days off to return to his family and Sicilian village, Calamo, so his wife and kids can finally meet his own family. Before he leaves, his boss (Armando Tine) at the factory (a native American from New Jersey) asks him to bring home a special package to his hometown's local Mafia boss, Don Vincenzo (Ugo Attanasio).

The first part of the film follows Nino's journey with them via train and boat, and Nino extolling the sites as they go. This part of the film really puts the viewer in the time and place, and one can feel the excitement of the journey as the northern Italian family of Alberto's accustom themselves to the backward rusticity of Sicily. Nino's father is a hotheaded rube whose hand was shot off, his mother is a fat prig whom Nino cannot even tell apart from an aunt, and his sister, Rosalia (Gabriella Conti) is an average looking girl cursed with a thin mustache. Initially, Marta is ill at ease and resents the family's cold treatment of her and the girls- and this highlights the North-South dichotomy of Italy that is as intense as that in America, but she eventually warms up. They pay a visit to Don Vincenzo, and his henchmen size Nino up as a possible shooter in a hit they have planned back in America. After Nino's father gets into a scrape with a man he has agreed to buy land from, after the landowner reneges on a deal and wants to raise the price, Don Vincenzo smoothes things out, and this endebts Nino, who is told to go on a hunting trip with old friends, to which Marta does no object, as she is now getting along with his family- especially Rosalia, whose mustache she waxes off.

Nino meets with one of Don Vincenzo's henchmen, Don Liborio (Carmelo Oliviero), who brings him to the boss's car. There he is told that he must do a favor for the don, to which he agrees. He is then told he must give a letter to someone, but is told he needs to be put in a crate. He is then flown to America, although we only see black with streaks of light, as we see Nino's POV from inside the same crate, where he arrives in New York City, meets some American gangsters, gives the letter to the boss, who rips it up, and is told he must take out a rival boss who is to be shot in a barber's chair, in a shop in North Bergen, New Jersey. The scenes in New York all take place in the last 20 minutes of the film, and, after we see him shoot the other boss, all we see is Nino leave, blackened inside the crate again, sneaking into his wife's bed in the family home, tormented by the memory of the killing, and then back at his job, returning a pen he'd inadvertently taken at film's start (showing he's really a good man, despite the film's ending sequences), then walking in his factory, away from the camera, in a complete 180° turn from the film's opening industrial scenes. The very abruptness of the violence and aftermath greatly aid the film, for it leaves the viewer as irresolute as Nino likely is.

Produced by Dino De Laurentiis, Mafioso plays to and subverts some stereotypes, and is an enjoyable film to watch, but not particularly insightful. Yes, it puts one in a time and place very well, but, just as one can say that *Moby-Dick* is not merely about 19th Century whaling, one cannot say that *Mafioso* is about anything other than a narrow slice of Sicilian culture. Part of this falls on the screenplay, co-written by Rafael Azcona, Bruno Caruso, Marco Ferreri, Agenore Incrocci, and Furio Scarpelli. The fact that five heads went into the screenplay accounts for why the film tends to lack a focus. This actually aids the film, in some ways, as Nino is a bit of a dim-witted bon vivant, but it also disallows the film from rising above mere entertainment- with the exception of the realistic last twenty minutes. The film's score, by Nino Rota and Piero Piccioni, is good, but not one of Rota's more memorable efforts, and the cinematography and editing, by Armando Nannuzzi and Nino Baragli, respectively, is merely solid. Lattuada shows, in his direction of all this, that he was a competent director, but one lacking a vision, a daemon, a driving force. The film is shown in a 1.85:1 aspect ration, and the streaming version I saw on Netflix had bright red subtitles which contrasted against the black and white film. What's unusual about this is that the film is a release of the Criterion Collection, which usually stupidly puts borderless white subtitles on its black and white films. This fact suggests that the subtitles were either remastered for Netflix or possibly the original subtitles for the film (which I doubt). Initially I thought that English dubbing would work, but, once in America, with the local goombahs speaking Italian and English, this film shows why and when subtitling is needed.

On the plus side are scenes of humor in Nino's clan; his moments on the beach with his old friends, who are unmarried, unemployed, and build female bodies out of sand to salivate over (apparently porno magazines were too modern for this area of the world, in those days), a chicken that gets under Marta's and Nino's bed; Nino's encounter with and fear of a black cat just moments before Don Liborio shows up to take him to Don Vincenzo; his joy in New York upon seeing a Sophia Loren movie poster for *Boccaccio 70*; and his meeting up with a drunken black man in New Jersey, who has been tossed out of a white bar because he wants to use the whites only restroom, on the way to his hit. On the negative side is the fact that Nino seems to have blithely believed he had risen above his roots. We hear how he has regrets for unnamed things he was forced to do as a kid, but then he seems unaware that he is in a no-win situation and being sent on a hit, even though, from the moment Don Liborio escorts him to Don Vincenzo's car, any reasonable man should have known what was going on, including the ruse of the letter delivery. Finally, driving from New York to New Jersey, with the American hoods, he wises up, and when asked the name of his daughters, he gives false names in a vain attempt to possibly shield his offspring from repercussions, should something go wrong. Yet, with a past in gangsterism, and at a shooting gallery with Don Liborio, one would think Nino would be smart enough to know he is being sized up, and shoot poorly, but his pride gives him away, and this leads him to his denouement.

As stated, the film is rife with good moments, as well as some not so good ones, but, overall, *Mafioso* is merely an interesting and pleasant film to watch. Not all things need be masterpieces to have value, and this film falls into that category, for better or worse.

DVD Review Of *The Conformist*
Copyright © by Dan Schneider, 2012

If there were to be a dictionary image associated with the word *heavyhanded* it might as well have a still image from Italian director Bernardo Bertolucci's 1970 film *The Conformist* (*Il Conformista*), for, despite its critical claims as a masterpiece, and the raving reviews of almost all the critics I could find with reviews online, it's really a startlingly banal and vacant film. In fact, an even more apt pegging of the film than *heavyhanded* might be the well worn phrase *style over substance*. Regardless of the ways to describe the film's failures it is absolutely stunning how such a mediocre, at best, film draws such raves from people supposedly employed to be able to see such obvious flaws.

First, there has never been a great film that did not have an accompanying great screenplay. Despite its visual nature, film is far more an extension of literature into the visual than photography into the narrative. And, despite raves for the cinematography of Vittorio Storaro, the film is not nearly as daring nor memorable a visual treat as is propounded. Yes, there are some nice visuals of nature, some canted shots, but *The Third Man* it is not. And, the screenplay by Bertolucci, adapted from Alberto Moravia's 1947 novel of the same name, is a dull stew of predictable action, trite characters, and huge gaps in plotting and logic. Add in some poor editing choices, by Franco Arcalli and Bertolucci, that often lose a viewer as to the chronology and import of events, and, well, the film is saved from being a total mess only by the best cinematography, the often unintendedly humorous pomp, and the magnificent use of 1930s fascist Art Deco shooting locations. The film's psychology for its characters, its silly sexuality, its achingly forced simulacrum of Expressionism, and a myriad of other bathetic and contrived conceits makes the film, at best, an archetype of late 1960s and early 1970s post-New Wave Eurotrash Cinema- not as bad as the pap proffered by such Eurotrash schlockmeisters as Jean Cocteau, Pier Paolo Pasolini, nor Luis Bunuel, but certainly not good, much less great. And it lacks any of the silliness that made Luchino Visconti's over the top *The Damned*, released just a year before, such campy fun.

The film follows a sexually and ethically addled Roman, Marcello Clerici (Jean-Louis Trintignant), who we eventually, hamhandedly, and predictably, has a homosexual past that involves murder of an older man- a chauffeur named Lino (Pierre Clémenti), who wanted to sexually abuse him, as a teenager in World War One. Catholic guilt over the sodomy and murder drive the upper crust bourgeois Clerici into a bestial lifestyle, or so we are told; one unabated by his parents- an insane and institutionalized father, and a morphine addict mother who sleeps with her Japanese chauffeur. Via ill wrought flashbacks and their poorly structured insertion into the current narrative, we piece together Clerici's desire to 'be normal.' Hence the film's title, as he enters into the Fascist Party's secret police, at the urging of Italo (José Quaglio), his blind mentor in Fascism, as an assassin who, during the 1930s, tracks down and kills Anti-Fascists. We soon learn he is assigned to take out an Italian exile in Paris- his former professor, Luca Quadri (Enzo Tarascio), while on his honeymoon to his petty bourgeois bride, Giulia (Stefania Sandrelli)- a girl whose idea of scandal is having had a six year affair with a 60 year old family friend. Along with them is a co-conspirator and enforcer named Manganiello (Gastone Moschin), whom Giulia seems remarkably oblivious of. Upon arriving in Paris, Clerici predictably falls in love, at first sight, with the professor's beautiful blond wife, Anna (Dominique Sanda), who, despite knowing he's an assassin, reciprocates almost immediately. Equally predictably, Anna is a bisexual with lesbian designs on Giulia.

Of course, none of this comes to any fruition, but is served to the viewer merely as an aperitif, of sorts, for, in the end, after whining and wanting to back out, before being physically dominated by Manganiello, in a quasi-homoerotic embrace, Clerici organized a hit on Anna and Quadri on a deserted country road. In doing so, it is revealed that Clerici has access to at least half a dozen knife and gun wielding thugs who quickly and brutally dispatch both, making the bulk of the film's cloak and dagger seem utterly superfluous, both narratively and psychologically. We do get the film's signature moment, though, when Anna runs to Clerici's car, sees him inside, and bangs on his window, finally realizing that her golden sex means nothing to such a man.

The film then flashes forward a few years, to 1943, and the fall of Mussolini's government. Marcello and Giulia have a small daughter, and he seems to have eminently succeeded as a conformist. He gets a call from Italo, wanders the streets of Rome, and overhears an old homosexual trying to seduce a young homeless man. Clerici confronts the homosexual, whom he recognizes as Lino, having survived the gunshot wound from Clerici's youth. This sends Clerici into insanity, where he denounces Lino as a homosexual, a Fascist, and the murderer of the Quadris. He then denounces Italo, as a mob of Anti-fascists take Italo away. Shaken, Clerici sinks into mental illness in the streets, near a fire, and has sexual visions.

Yes, that's it. The ending is original to Bertolucci's screenplay, not the source novel, and it shows, for the novel's ending had a more realistic than psychosexual ending that is emblematic of all the film's failings- from a Freudian slavishness to a hypermoralistic dudgeon, and, given the film's style over substance quotient, one would have hoped Bertolucci would have, at least, in the moments that he is trying to make a point, make deep and relevant points, and employ them well. Instead, this facile film would rather show the obvious point to be made, and do so in even a more overt manner. And that it does all this with stereotypes- the sexually conflicted anti-hero, the naïf wife, the intellectual good European man of Socialism, the Fascist thug, the hedonistic mother, etc.. is all the worse for the viewer. Bertolucci allows no nuance, no subtlety, and his characters never converse, they speechify, or declaim banalities. The absolute worst moment of the film comes when Clerici tries to worm his way in Quadri's good graces. Until that point, the professor is rightly suspicious of Clerici as an assassin, and does not even recall him. Then, Clerici dims some blinds, and remarks of how influenced he was by the professor's philosophic explanation of Plato's Cave as an analogy for the sweep of Fascism across Europe. Aside from the utter simplemindedness of the metaphor, applied to 1930s Europe, there is simply no way that Plato's Cave could, even then, hope to impress a college student as a deep and interesting idea, in its own right- much less be seen as a potential thesis any philosophy professor would care to read. But, on top of these two absurdities, Bertolucci has the professor totally swallow his student's fawning, embrace him into his inner circle, and declaim Clerici as his prized student, whereas mere minutes before, in the film's narrative, he had absolutely no idea who Clerici was.

That *The Conformist* won a number of film festival awards is remarkable because it simply is not a good film. It's not terrible, but it is utterly forgettable. Even its score, by Georges Delerue, is overwrought. The DVD, an Extended Edition (111 minutes in length), by Paramount, is shown in a 1.66:1 aspect ratio, and has no film commentary. It has 3 small featurettes that, in toto, add up to almost 40 minutes of Bertolucci and his crew talking of the film's making: aspects such as the cast, the filming, and the adaptation. It's a solid set, but the best part of the package comes in the fact that the film has a number of dubbed language options, and I watched it in English. This option again proves how vastly superior dubbing is to subtitles in foreign film. Yet, there was a brief scene where the dubbing went away and we saw the film in Italian, with highly readable gold subtitles. The reason for this is told in the third featurette, which explains why the DVD is called an Extended Edition. The scene of Clerici and Italo meeting a bunch of (*get ready for this*) blind Fascists who meet in a cellar (*underground- see, get the metaphor?*), was cut by Bertolucci, for American distributors because it was not part of Moravia's original novel. And, frankly, it's a rare example of suits making a good film decision by accident because the film absolutely has no need for the scene.

By contrast, all the critics who have praised this shiny bauble of nihility and banal preachiness need to hang their heads in shame. No, *The Conformist* is not one of the worst films ever made- just a fairly generically bad Eurotrash film of its era, but its title is far more apt for those clueless critics than it is for the film's protagonist, who might have more aptly been called *The Cipher*.

Film Review Of *Electra*
Copyright © by Dan Schneider, 2012

   Watching Greek filmmaker Michael Cacoyannis's (aka Mihalis Kakogiannis, who also directed *Zorba The Greek*) 1962 black and white film *Electra* (*Elektra* or *Ilektra*) is a study in the power of archetypes, for the film is short on any real internal diegesis and long on, as well as dependent upon, a prior knowledge of the particulars of the mythos surrounding the Agamemnon-Orestes-Electra tales. There is nothing in the way of character development, shading, and the action propelled forth at the virgin eyes of a neophyte viewer, yet, by the end of this hour and 52 minute film, one is aware that there is quality in this work, and it is more than the mere technical skill needed to being this film to the screen.

   For those not in on the mythos, this film follows the return of Agamemnon (Theodoros Dimitriou) from the Trojan War, to his kingdom of Mycenae, only to be betrayed and murdered by his wife, Clytemnestra (Aleka Katselli), and her lover Aegisthus (Fivos Razi), who takes over as the new king. Held as a prisoner in her own home is the young Electra (Irene Papas), while her brother Orestes (Yannis Fertis), is spirited away by his teacher, still loyal to Agamemnon. And this is not just my recap, but the recap of the tales in the first five minutes of the film, shot beautifully, at sunset, on a high plain, in riveting black and white.

   We then fast forward through time, to see a grown Electra cut off her locks, toss them in front of her mother, and accept banishment and marriage to a peasant (Notis Peryalis) who does not touch her. There, she lives in celibacy, as her husband tends his fields and her needs are met by a literal Greek chorus of servant girls. Meanwhile, Orestes has been wandering for years, plotting his return (foretold to Electra by the Delphic Oracle) to his throne, and the death of Aegisthus, accompanied by his friend Pylades (Takis Emmanuel). After little action and much emotional agon, Orestes stumbles upon his sister (who can deny that Classic mythology is the precursor of modern soap opera?), but dismisses her as a slave girl. He and Pylades soon end up at Electra's husband's home, and are taken for assassins. Electra tries to hide, and Orestes does not reveal who he is.

   Of course, he soon relents- only after his nature is revealed by the now aged teacher (Manos Katrakis) who saved him from Aegisthus as a child, and the reunited siblings quickly plot the murders of their stepfather and mother. First protesting, Orestes agrees to take out Aegisthus, which he does, at a vineyard Bacchanalia. Then, Electra waits for Clytemnestra to come, for she has had the teacher go tell her mother that she has had her first child and wants Clytemnestra to attend to some rituals for her. Unaware her husband has been slain by her son, Clytemnestra arrives at dawn and she and her daughter exchange backhistory (the equivalent of flashbacks) to educate the viewer on the original myth, and then, after luring her mother into her husband's home, Orestes does the deed and- guess what?- after they kill their mother, both siblings regret the deed. Even the subjects of the kingdom, who celebrated Orestes' killing of Aegisthus, turn against them. They stone the house, until Orestes, Pylades, and Electra exit. More weeping and wailing ensue. Electra and Orestes wander aimlessly in despair, in different directions. Pylades follows his master, until told to tend to Electra, whom he then follows, as the lead Greek chorus girl (Theano Ioannidou) bemoans the fact that never before, and never again will a family be so blessed and cursed as this one.

   Now, if you are not exactly at the edge of your seat, don't be concerned. The characters in the myth are not really meant to be individuals, they are meant to be generic, and thus their zombie state is natural. The characters in Greek tragedies are all guided by the principle of *What if?*- meaning, what if a daughter, mourning her father, murdered by her mother and her mother's lover. Were to plot revenge with her long lost brother- well, what would happen if….that were so? And, because the magic hour filming, as well as filtered day for night scenes, works so well in constructing a fug of drama, it somehow sucks in even viewers who may be wholly ignorant of the whats and wherefores.

On a technical level the film, shown in a 1.66:1 aspect ratio, is brilliant: the cinematography by Walter Lasally is gorgeous, and the positioning of the actors' miens prefigures some of the work Ingmar Bergman would indulge in just a few years later. The editing, by Leonidas Antonakis is likewise first rate. The subtitles are unfortunately white and borderless, and, if streaming on a regular television, they are cut off. But on big screen tv's and computers this is not an issue. Taken together, the film is a master course in composing spare tableaux, and, if Bergman took much from Cacoyannis's peer into the visage of the peeled ape, then Cacoyannis was channeling the same God-like impassive gaze upon the macro things at hand, for the film pulls in and out of the dilemmas human and often sweeps around onto the high dry plains that these acts take place upon. Also impressive is the film's score, by Mikis Theodorakis, which is ominous and deific in its pomp, when needed, and subtle and mournful when required. The acting is generally solid, but the reality is that what is given as 'acting' in a film like this is going to be considered, in any other dramatic work- of cinema or not- over the top and scenery chewing. Yet, even with this caveat, the best performance in the film does not come from the titular lead character's portrayer, Irene Papas- who would go on to become one of Greece's top film stars, but from Aleka Katselli, whose Clytemnestra- especially in her speech justifying the murder of her husband, shows depth, logic and range, even as the viewer is aware that none of this will translate into her escaping her death for, no matter the humanity infused into Clytemnestra, she is, was, and always will be Clytemnestra. And this is where Cacoyannis is at his best, as the film's screenwriter, for he takes the classic myth, the assorted plays (Sophocles, Euripides, etc.), and strips them of pomp and circumstance, then tosses the ancient against the then in vogue European tendency to use harsh landscapes, especially in black and white films, as a de facto character in the film- Bergman, Antonioni, and many others indulged this tendency, but since this film is saddled with a several millennia old tale, it reinvigorates much of what should be stale, with the synesthesia of visuals and primal memory, or, as the usually stolid film critic for the New York Times, Bosley Crowther, quite presciently wrote:

> Where previous attempts to make movies from the Greek classics have generally mired in the heavy going of too much declamation of the original poetic dialogue, this film avoids that dangerous pitfall by going to the other extreme and swinging wide of a form of presentation that is physically hitched to the structure of the stage.
>
> Clearly, Mr. Cacoyannis knows you can't photograph words, that a medium as visual as motion pictures must not put too much dependence on the ear. Also, he sees that the contours of the drama in the Greek tragedies are so massive and elemental that they may be suggested and impressed upon the eye with a proper and tasteful presentation of graphic images.
>
> Thus, he has made this "Electra" a powerful address to the eyes. He has taken his company outdoors and set it against the countryside, against great sweeping vistas of rugged landscape and eloquent stretches of sky.

It should also be noted that Cacoyannis highlights the violence immanent in the tale by never showing it, only the aftermath. This actually heightens the emotions for, such as the scene where Electra spews her venom at the corpse of Aegisthus, it acts as a de facto substitute for what we have not seen her brother do. It's only one unfortunate angle of a shot of Electra above Aegisthus's dead head that lessens the scene as we see the live actor's jugular pulsing, thus giving away the moment as a fiction diegetically, as well as really.

Nonetheless, aside from that moment the scene and technique work well. Call it *zombie formalism*, or maybe even *zombie naturalism*, but whatever you call it, it works, and even a day or two later, the film sticks with you, and increases in the mind, in terms of power, almost like the long films and scenes in Bela Tarr films are naturally shrunk to their essences in memory. A similar 'magic,' for lack of a better term- oh, here's one: 'skill,' inhabits the very scenes that Cacoyannis impresses his ages old emotions and narrative against upon. Be it harsh terrain, of earth or soul, *Electra* graces and tugs the entrails- almost to greatness unadulterated, although, when one analyzes too closely it falls apart. But, fear not, for the centrifuge of memory acometh, and it be not ill!

Film Review Of *The Trojan Women*
Copyright © by Dan Schneider, 2013

In 1971, Greek director Michael Cacoyannis released the middle film of his trilogy of Greek classic plays- his adaptation of Euripides' *The Trojan Women*. Unlike the earlier *Electra* and later *Iphigenia*, this color film was shot and recorded in English (from the Edith Hamilton translation), because three of its four leading ladies were non-Greek actresses. The 105 minute long film starred American actress Katharine Hepburn as Hecuba, British actresses Vanessa Redgrave as Andromache, Canadian actress Geneviève Bujold as Cassandra, and Greek actress Irene Papas as Helen of Troy.

Unshockingly, the best, yet briefest, performance is given by Papas, as the beauty whose capture by Paris of Troy led to the Trojan War. The bulk of the film takes place at a prisoner of war camp outside the sacked and looted Troy, as the Greeks plan their return with the captured Trojan women as potential slaves and lovers. Shot as a spare, post-Apocalyptic series of dramatic monologues, the play actually works, for the most part, despite the uncinematic nature of the play. Fortunately, Cacoyannis decided to drop the intrusion of the Olympian gods in the drama, and focused, instead, on the four main women, and their literal Greek chorus of nameless Trojan women.

Some critics have criticized the film for a lack of realism, and, to a degree, they have a point, as much of the speechifying by the non-Greek actresses is accompanied by an almost Shakespearean delivery of lines, as if not being captured offhandedly on camera, but being declaimed to an invisible audience. But, at another level, this sort of criticism utterly fails, because the soliloquizing of the characters is far from the only thing that is unrealistic in this film. In fact, had a more realistic approach to acting been taken, it would have stood out in great contrast to all the visual razzle-dazzle Cacoyannis employs, from the subjective camera eye that seeps into the characters it embodies- from shots of lying down in a slave caravan to being tossed off a cliff. Then there is the freeze frame sequence that starts the film, wherein the frozen frames of the sack of Troy are rendered from color to sepia, accompanied by a voice of God-like narration. Staggered shots of faces and partial shots of faces also display the jagged frame of mind of the speakers, individually, and in chorus. All in all, it's a film that both follows the classic Cacoyannis formula, yet, when needed, utterly dashes it, to serve the needs of the moment and the film.

The four major female characters all get their moments in the un, as they await their post-War fates. Hecuba, the Queen of the Trojans and mother of Hector, Troy's most famed warrior, killed in battle, laments the passage of the past. Her daughter in law, Andromache, widow of Hector, and mother of his son Astyanax (Alberto Sanz), laments the Greeks' decision to slaughter her son. Cassandra, Hecuba's daughter, later to become the unbelieved prophetess, battles with insanity as she is shipped off to Greece. Helen of Troy, Hecuba's other daughter in law, via her son Paris, waits to see if she will live, as the rest of the Trojan women lust for her death. After their moments in the sun, so to speak, their fates are all made known with the arrival of Talthybius (Brian Blessed), the messenger of the Greek king, Agamemnon. The arrival of Menelaus (Patrick Magee), King of Sparta, only confirms their fates. The film then ends with the burning and destruction of Troy.

All in all, a fairly spare plot, but, as with all films of substance, the what of the plot is not nearly as important as the how, and, as mentioned, Cacoyannis makes a bravura usage of dramatic pauses, technical trickery, and a knowledge of the general outlines of the Greek myths undergirding this film, to make it, if not a great film, outright, certainly an excellent one. Perhaps the lone negative of the film is, surprisingly, the abundance of black rags as clothing worn by Hecuba and the other imprisoned Trojan women. By contrast, shots of Helen's beauty, and her white clothing, when she takes a seductive bath in a pot of water, giving glimpses of her shapely body, stand in direct contrast to the black clothing otherwise omnipresent.

Mikis Theodorakis's musical score is very apt and allows the viewer to settle into an emotional state that the images play virtuosically off of. Alfio Contini's cinematography is stark, moody, and evokes a Robinson Jeffers like power in how the landscapes reflect the power of the female laments. This contrast of the male imagery and female regret is a powerful tension throughout the film, and shows up how much such tension is missed in standard sandals and swords epics filmed in similar climes.

The Trojan Women is a film that, with a few tweaks, here and there, could have been a film of truly epic and great proportions, but Cacoyannis deserves all sorts of credit for the film he has wrought. Overall, the critics missed the boat on this film, likely by falling into one of the oldest critical traps there is: reviewing not the film they actually had in front of them, but the film they felt *should be* in front of them, given all the talent amassed behind and in front of the camera. By that approach, few films can be accorded their due. But, sans that flaw, *The Trojan Women* stands as an admirable film, one with far more pluses than minuses, and definitely one to watch if one is interested in Greek cinema, and classic Greek drama.

Film Review Of *Iphigenia*
Copyright © by Dan Schneider, 2013

 Greek film director Michael Cacoyannis (aka Mihalis Kakogiannis, who also directed
Zorba The Greek) is one of those filmmakers whose work is almost instantly
recognizable from any ten to twelve second clip, for his portrayal of ancient Greek life,
especially, is like no other films in the sword and sandal genre. In fact, even linking his
mythical films to the sword and sandal epics that were produced in Hollywood and
mainstream European film in the mid-20th Century, is somewhat of a blatant diss to this
man's creations. Following up on watching his near great black and white 1962 film,
Electra, I took in his 130 minute long, 1977 color masterwork, *Iphigenia* (*Ifigeneia*), and,
frankly, there's a reason why the later film is greater than the earlier film, and that is
because *Iphigenia* has all of *Electra*'s masterly pros, and none of its cons.
 The acting in *Electra* is almost rigidly formal, whereas in *Iphigenia*, it is real. The
Greeks shown in this film are a step above Neandertals- barely. They stink and sweat and
look disgusting. These are not the children of the gods, but the barbarians they claim to
despise. They are raw and bloodthirsty, even as some do mouth some of the pieties that
can be found in the classic plays of Euripedes, but Cacoyannis wisely realizes and
humanizes the characters. They rage, but it is not a rage borne of drama, but of knowing
they are mortal and resenting the sacrifices asked of them, including the biggest of all:
King Agamemnon's daughter Iphigenia, to sate the gods and allow the Greeks winds
enough to journey to Troy and end the Trojan War.
 Ostensibly, little happens in the film, save the revelation that Agamemnon must
summon his wife and children so that his daughter's sacrifice can ensure victory. There
are no great battle scenes, but the use of hundreds, if not thousands, of real life extras
shows how lacking in power CGI scenes of crowds can be, for there is a real sense of
dread and claustrophobia some of the scenes impart that one never gets in large crowd
shots from CGI films. This version of the Iphigenia myth is the more 'human' one,
wherein Iphigenia's final fate is not one of a last minute rescue, hence the earlier scenes
take on a greater poignancy, as Iphigenia (Tatiana Papamoschou, who does not even
appear in her titular film until 20 minutes in) pleads for her life, only to realize she is
doomed, and accepts her fate, despite the courage of her supposedly intended husband,
Achilles (Panos Mihalopoulos), in being willing to die for her.
 Aside from the ambiguous ending, the film diverges from the classical plays of
Euripides in a few other ways. There is the addition of realism by bringing forth
characters like Odysseus (Christos Tsagas) and Calchas (Dimitris Aronis), high priest of
Artemis' temple, who were merely mentioned in the play, to the subtraction of formal
dramatic elements like a Greek chorus, so that the testosteronic chants of the stranded
Greek army is foregrounded. Their chants emerge after the winds subside, thus stranding
the army short of its goal of Troy. In order to summon the winds, Agamemnon is directed
by an oracle that his first born daughter's life need be sacrificed, to show that he is as
willing as his men to shed blood. Of course, his wife, Clytemnestra (Irene Papas- who
plays Electra- the daughter who kills Clytemnestra in the earlier film), reviles him when
she finds out, because Agamemnon had killed her first husband and made her bear him
these children that she feels he will destroy. This sacrifice of Iphigenia, although told in a
later film, explain much of the motivation for Agamemnon's murder at the start of the
earlier film, *Electra*.
 As for the larger tale? Helen, the Spartan queen of King Menelaus (Costas Carras) has
been abducted by Paris, the son of Trojan King Priam. Menelaus asks his brother,
Agamemnon (Kostas Kazakos), to lead the war against Troy, to rescue Helen, who never

appears in the film, is Clytemnestra's half-sister, and hated by Clytemnestra as a slatternly demigoddess. None of this is explicit in the film, but even a slight background of the mythos helps explain much of the tale, which, even sans this knowledge, is remarkably lucid and emotionally powerful, despite its unrealistic nature, precisely because it is shown so naturalistically. The only non-naturalistic element to the film is the fog shrouded ending, but the final shot of the film- a closeup of Clytemnestra's rage filled eyes, is a devastatingly apt image to foreshadow the things to come, as shown in the earlier film.

  The technical aspects of Cacoyannis's film are very well done, and the pans of the landscape take on a symbolism that lesser cinematography could not evoke. The land, in essence, becomes a character, as the rocks, wind, barren hillsides, empty ships, waves, sun, unused weapons, and other things, all have moments where they are imbued with depths a lesser filmmaker would and could not achieve, and would not even think of attempting. Also, many shots show a look on a character's face. But now what he or she is seeing, suggesting that there is an internal world of the film that we, the audience, are not shown. The best example of this is at film's end when the mists shroud Iphigenia, and a regretful Agamemnon runs up the steps to ostensibly save her. We see him look at us, the audience, in the position where Iphigenia would be, but we never see the reverse shot. Only fog is left. Has Calchas sacrificed her? Or have the gods interceded and spared her, like the aborted Biblical sacrifice of Isaac by Abraham? The film scoring, by Mikis Theodorakis, is, at moments, devastatingly portentous, and at others softly affectionate. There is never misdirection, but it is definitely a classical use of scoring to heighten the already moving image or scene. Similarly, as mentioned, the editing, by Takis Yanopoulos, and the cinematography, by Giorgos Arvanitis, is top notch. Cacoyannis's adaptation from Euripedes' *Iphigenia At Aulis*, is also stellar, in its wise choices of when to remain true to the original, and when to modernize the tale. The film is shown in a 1.66:1 aspect ratio. About the only negative to the film, technical or otherwise, is the poor quality of day for night shots, possibly due to poor filters or even just degradation of the film stock over the decades. The film was nominated for a Best Foreign Film Academy Award, as well as the Palm D'Or at the Cannes Film Festival, as well as numerous nominations and awards at other film festivals.

  Overall, *Iphigenia* stands as proof that the very oldest and most archetypal tales can still be fodder for the most modern artistic media, and Cacoyannis shows that he was one of the masters of this sort of make it new approach to art. For anyone who is intimidated when confronted with the Greek classics, Cacoyannis provides not only a good entry point into a lost world, but a great entry point into the filmic art at its most essential. *Iphigenia* is essential *and* great.

Film Review Of *The Cherry Orchard*
Copyright © by Dan Schneider, 2013

Having watched a number of Michael Cacoyannis's films dealing with Greek subject matter, and in the Greek language, it was interesting to see what he would do when given non-Greek subject matter (the Russian play, *The Cherry Orchard*, by Anton Chekhov), and filmed in a language other than Greek (English), as the film was a joint production of Greece, France, and Germany, and starred English actors.

In short, while it's a good, solid film, and a fairly faithful adaptation of a great play, the film itself lacks the very elements that made Cacoyannis's Classical Greek films great: depth and great visuals. The screenplay was adapted by Cacoyannis, and the 140 minute film does not drag.

As in the play, the film follows the financial descent of a Russian noblewoman, Lyobov Andreyevna Ranevskaya (Charlotte Rampling). The film opens with something not in the play, and that is her leaving her life in Paris behind, to attend to the auctioning off of her Cherry Orchard estate, because a faithless lover of hers swindled her. Returning with her is her daughter, Anya (Tushka Bergen), she encounters her equally lazy and bourgeois brother, Leonid (Alan Bates), who is being advised by his lawyer, Lopakhin (Owen Teale), who is also the son of former serfs on the estate, that the estate cannot be sustained without it being sold off or broken into pieces and rented out as a vacation resort. Lopakhin has the hots for the mistress's oldest daughter Varya (Katrin Cartlidge), but refuses to act upon it.

Most of the film plays out like an episode of Masterpiece Theater, in both the best and worst senses of that claim, with social observations, melodramas, and the like which, at their best, reveal the political situations of the era (late Czarist Russia), and, at their worst, reveal none of the comic elements of the play, which achieves its own greatness on the interplay between satire and real drama. When the satire is good, it is quite good- see the scenes with the insane butler, Feers (Michael Gough), or the wacky governess, Charlotta (Frances De La Tour), who has no real clue as to her own past, but when it is bad it is, well, just nonexistent- see the trite character of Pyotr (Andrew Howard), the social rebel cum anarchist who is in love with the beautiful younger daughter, Anya (Tushka Bergen). Pyotr flounders because his opinions are so stale and trite, even pre-Communist revolution that it's clear Chekhov saw him as comic relief, yet the film never displays him as such, and it's absurd to think Anya could ever be attracted to him, as she seems the most intelligent and level-headed of the lot of them.

The real lesson of the story, and film, is not that the future lies with Pyotr the dreamer, but with Lopakhin, the doer. It is he who is the victor over his family's former masters, even as he has generously tried to help them throughout. When they refuse his help and advice, he makes them obsolete, even by never working up the courage to ask for Varya's hand in marriage. But, why should he? He is the future, even in today's Russia. Varya and her clan are the past. The play ends with Feers seemingly dying in the abandoned estate as all the others leave, and the woodsmen chop down the trees, whose images and sounds echo those within the former nobles who, have made a tidy sum, with Leonid getting a banking job with a good salary, to boot. This revolution, so to speak, is a far cry from the one that a few decades later would start off a century of bloodlust in the name of socialism.

Technically, the film lacks the archetypal images and musical punctuations that dominate Cacoyannis's Classical films, although the music of Tchaikovsky is used very well. The acting is all first rate, especially from Rampling, Bergen, and Teale, yet, despite everything playing well, the parts are all better than the whole. The cinematography, by Aris Stavrou, is solid but unspectacular, as is Takis Hadzis's editing.

   This 1999 film version of *The Cherry Orchard* is worth a watch, if only for the writing and acting, but, as a film, it is nothing special, which is a shame, because the source play really is.

DVD Review of *Pigs And Battleships*
Copyright © by Dan Schneider, 2010

Watching Japanese director Shohei Imamura's black and white breakthrough comedy-drama film, from 1961, *Pigs And Battleships* (*Buta To Gunkan*, aka *The Flesh Is Hot*), is an interesting experience because, even though half a century old, it is still almost infinitely fresher and more innovative than the ill wrought and ill written action and thriller films that routinely get greenlighted nowadays. And, at a mere 108 minutes in length it packs a hell of a good story into a relatively short time frame.

The film is ostensibly about the life and times of a low rung wannabe yakuza gangster, Kinta (Hiroyuki Nagato), trying to work his way up the ranks of the underworld that controls the rackets outside of the United States Naval Base at Yokosuka, a Japanese seaport. He finds himself unable or unwilling to change his life for the love of a beautiful girl named Haruko (Jitsuko Yoshimura), who spends most of the film as his ignored conscience, trying to get him jobs in legitimate businesses, even as she tries to extricate herself from an uncaring family life and a dead end job as a barmaid. Instead, Kinta shows loyalty only to his direct Boss, who is merely an underboss in the local operation, run by a never seen Big Boss, who seems to be in cahoots with both American mobsters from Hawaii and Chinese gangsters. Kinta's boss, Tetsu (Tetsuro Tamba), is a hypochondriac who spends most of the film believing he has stomach cancer, which is really just an ulcer, and wishing to die (a nice twist and nod to Akira Kurosawa'a brilliant *Ikiru*), while his idiotic underlings fret over making payments to their overboss so that they can keep control of the local pig farm racket. Kinta is assigned to both care for the pigs and take the fall for the Big Boss if their plans to eliminate a rival gang's boss fall through.

Meanwhile, the locals have been converted to idealizing almost all things American. Capitalism is thriving, and even Haruko contemplates life as a whore, or at least a Yank sailor's mistress. By film's end, though, almost all the main characters end up dead or vanquished. Kinta's gang turns on the overboss's men, and they try to set Kinta up as the fall guy. Instead, he grabs a machine gun, shoots up the nearby red light district, and releases hundreds of pigs to run wild through the street. Cops come and the pigs manage to maul and/or trample many of the gangsters on both sides, while Kinta is shot and bleeds to death. Haruko, who was planning to leave for another city, hears of the 'incident,' and immediately suspects Kinta's involvement. When she sees his corpse carried away she is inconsolable, yet also angry. The last few minutes of the film follow her in the aftermath, as she sets her life in order, with the film ending as she walks steadfastly away from her past and family and into the future, a shot that is almost a direct quotation from Kenji Mizoguchi's 1936 film, *Osaka Elegy*, in which that film's heroine, also leaves her shattered life behind, ending that film walking off into her future, a quarter of a century earlier.

The DVD, from The Criterion Collection, is a solid offering, part of a three DVD set called *Pigs, Pimps, And Prostitutes*, along with *The Insect Woman* and *Intentions Of Murder*. The transfer of the film, shown in a 2.35:1 aspect ration, is virtually flawless. There are no noticeable scratches nor imperfections. The camera work, by cinematographer Sinsaku Himeda, is electrifying, at its best, and interesting all other times, right from the film's opening pan through Haruko's rape scene by three American sailors (who sing *I've Been Working On The Railroad* as an overhead shot of the hotel room they are in starts spinning relentlessly) up till the final pigs are unleashed ending. Even better is the great film scoring by Toshiro Mayazumi, who often has lengthy musical scenes, just to punctuate others with wildly ironic and jingoistic marches. The

DVD comes with no audio commentary, which is a shame, and, even worse, offers no English language dubbing. Fortunately, Criterion's white font subtitles, which so often are unreadable against pale backgrounds in black and white films, are saved by the widescreen black bars, which make for, at least, a readable contrast for the subtitles. The screenplay, by Hisashi Yamauchi, adapted from a novel by Kazu Otsuka, is actually very good, especially so at balancing humor with action. It's a major break from the many contemporary dramas made by Kurosawa and Yasujiro Ozu, whom Imamura apprenticed under as an assistant director, and is laced with both subtle and not so subtle political jabs at both American and Japanese authority figures (starting with his film's opening claim that the film's story is 'entirely fictional'). As for other features, there is an hour long documentary called *Imamura: The Freethinker*, which appeared on the French television series, *Cinema De Notre Temps*. It's a solid profile of the man, but sort of skimps on filmic facts and scenes in favor of philosophy. There's also an interview with film critic and historian Tony Rayns, on the film. Again, solid, but nothing great, as it runs only a quarter hour. Why Criterion could not have gotten Rayns to do a commentary is beyond me. The only other feature is an insert booklet featuring an essay on the film by film critic Audie Bock. Of interest is that this film apparently got Imamura demoted from director status at his Nikkatsu studio, due to its poor critical and box office reception, and for a couple of years he worked on screenplays as a script doctor.

Yet, looking back a half a century later, this film scores well on almost all counts. Perhaps it is not a slam dunk great work of cinema, but it has good acting, a great script, great technical skills shown, and, as mentioned, is as fresh as any film can hope to be after five decades have passed. *Pigs And Battleships* is a terrific film, with both great comedic and dramatic moments, and possibly a great overall film, that signaled the rise of not only a talented new director from Japan, but also a new take on the way older Japanese filmmakers handled their subject matter. Imamura's influence still reverberates in the works of far lesser directors like Quentin Tarantino and his even lesser protégés; except that where Imamura used his technical skills to advance the narrative of his film, folks like Tarantino and company simply like to beat up people and blow things up, and that is the point of their films. Looking at the aftermath of the Haruko rape scene shows why Imamura snd the script are so good. Haruko schemes to steal the sailors' money, and in a lesser film she would have easily gotten away with it, providing the film's universe with a sense of ethics and justice. But, in this film, as in real life, Haruko is chased and caught by the American rapists, and she is taken to spend a night in jail, charged with theft and prostitution. Not giving in to easy outs is the sign of an artist that is good, and possibly on the way to greatness. *Pigs And Battleships* may have been his first encounter with such.

DVD Review of *The Insect Woman*
Copyright © by Dan Schneider, 2010

Of the three Shohei Imamura films included in the DVD set, *Pigs, Pimps, And Prostitutes*: *Pigs And Battleships*, *The Insect Woman*, and *Intentions Of Murder*, the last film, a black and white effort made in 1964, is clearly the least of the three, although it is still quite a goof film. *Intentions Of Murder* (赤い殺意 or *Akai Satsui* or *Unholy Desire*) lacks the satiric edge and humor of *Pigs And Battleships* and is missing the realistic drama of *The Insect Woman*. In this manner the trilogy resembles that of fellow Japanese filmmaker Hiroshi Teshigahara's <u>Pitfall</u>, <u>Woman In The Dunes</u>, and <u>The Face Of Another</u>; with an arguably great first film, a masterpiece second film, and a daring, but merely good finale, because the last film overreaches.

Intentions Of Murder is the longest film, at 153 minutes, and it could have shed 30-40 minutes with no great loss. It follows the life and times of a plump young housewife, Sadako Takahashi (Masumi Harukawa), in a northern Japanese city, Sendai, who ended up marrying her lecherous employer after he impregnated her (seen in flashback). His family still looks down on her, to the point that her son Masaru (an actor whose name is not available online nor in the DVD credits), is not even legally registered with Sadako as his mother. Early on, with her husband out of town, at a conference, Sadako is raped by a burglar, Hiraoko (Shigeru Tsuyuguchi), and after thoughts of noble suicide and eating, she decides to tough it out. Then, Hiraoko becomes a stalker, and rapes her again, only to declare his love for her. Meanwhile, Sadako's husband, Riichi (Kô Nishimura), a librarian, is having an affair with a thin, bespectacled co-worker, Miss Masuda (Yuko Kusonoki), who obsesses over him, and sets out to break up their marriage, claiming that she is his true wife because she has been his lover longer than he has even known Sadako. She stumbles upon Sadako's new man, Hiraoko, whom she mistakes as a willing lover of Sadako's, and intends to prove that she is as unfaithful as he is. Masuda does this so Riichi will leave Sadako and she can raise Masaru as her own. Riichi is almost as abusive to Sadako as Hiraoko, calling her fat and stupid at every opportunity, as well as being an unfaithful louse, despite his having asthma and being attended to by his wife at every occasion. He is a weak man, both physically and ethically. Yet, Sadako is mistreated by all the men in her life, including her bratty son, who disobeys her and even calls her fat.

But, things complex as Sadako finds out she is pregnant, and does not know if the fetus is her husband's or the rapist's. She takes a train to a doctor's office in a nearby town, and Hiraoko confronts her, claiming the fetus is his, and wanting her to run away to Tokyo with him. When she refuses he tries to push her off the train. But, he has a heart condition and takes pills for it. Hiraoko has a seizure and she pities him, giving him an ampule, thus saving his life, but making his fixation even greater. He then cons her to a hotel, to explain things, and this time she willingly has sex with him. She plans to bribe him into leaving her alone after Masuda tells him about the rapist, and Sadako denies all, which sets Riichi's lover off to prove Sadako is having 'an affair.' Sadako then plans to kill Hiraoko with a poisoned tea, after she goes off with him on a train to Tokyo, and they have to walk through snow after a derailment. Masuda follows, snapping photos the whole way. Sadako tries to poison the rapist, when they take shelter in a tunnel, but at the last minute knocks the cup out of his hand, and Hiraoko claims he knew it was poisoned because her hands were shaking. They kiss, but he has another attack, and loses his medicine in the snow. Sadako cannot find it and he dies. She panics and runs. Masuda finds the dead rapist and photographs him, and follows Sadako back on the rain to Sendai.

Leaving the train station, Sadako doubles over with pain, and is taken to a hospital, where she miscarries. Masuda, photographing everything, steps into the street to get the license plate of the ambulance, and is killed by a truck that slams her high into the air. It is a moment that is unexpected, humorous, and evokes a 'yeah, baby' feeling in the viewer because she, not Hiraoko, is the real villain of the piece, as the two abusive men are no match for Sadako's resilience. But, Riichi gets ahold of his lover's camera, via another coworker, develops the film, and sees photos of his wife, and confronts her with them. She denies most, and throws his accusations back at him, showing she knows of his adultery, and with whom. Riichi then tries to find out if the fetus was his or not, but is told it had been disposed of. The film ends with a lengthy epilogue, wherein the family reforming, Riichi getting promoted, and Sadako getting legal recognition as Masaru's mother.

Many feminists deride the notion that a woman could fall in love with a rapist (see the American soap opera *General Hospital* and the early 1980s controversy of the Luke and Laura rape and marriage), and this is the basis for much negative criticism of the film but not once does Sadako claim to love her rapist. Yes, she once gives in to willing sex, but only to get him to agree to end it. But, in reality, her abuse at the hands of Hiraoko is not much worse than that her husband, Riichi, inflicts on her, and it's clear she does not love him either. In fact, Sadako clearly shows that she has loathing for both men, and given the abuse many other people- male and female (her mother-in-law, played by Ranko Akagi) - have heaped on her, in her past (see via flashbacks) it's not unreasonable to assume she might wonder if the rapist could, indeed, offer her a better life. After all, she does not know what we do, that he is a dying loser musician who can barely make ends meet playing at strip clubs. The reality is that the rapist falls in love with his victim, and this is the unbelievable part. The film tries to lessen Hiraoko's guilt by claiming he only stole to pay for his medicine, and that the first rape occurred on the day he found out he was going to die. Given the simplicity of the character's makeup, there simply is little chance that he could love anyone but his own self-pitying self. The trope also fails not because of its essence, but its clumsy soap operatic execution. There is simply no need for much of the film's later cloak and dagger routines. It cheapens the real psychological issues that are affecting Sadako something that does not occur in the superior *The Insect Woman*.

The DVD, from The Criterion Collection, is a solid offering. The film is shown in a 2.35:1 aspect ratio, and virtually flawless. There are no noticeable scratches nor imperfections. Cinematographer Shinsaku Himeda employs many cinéma vérité tactics and interesting schemes, such as freeze-frames and voiceovers that were used in the earlier films, and the scoring, by Toshiro Mayazumi, is, as in the other films, excellent and well deployed to convey character strengths and flaws, not to lead the narrative. The two mix especially well in a late scene where Masuda is following Sadako and her rapist, and violins crescendo during a shaky handheld scene. Another virtuosic musical moment occurs after the first rape, where a cartoonish 'boing-boing' sound dominates the scene. The screenplay, by Imamura and Keiji Hasebe, from a story by Shinji Fujiwara, is solid, but tries to pack to much into the film and, as mentioned, veers too often into melodrama. The DVD comes with no audio commentary and offers no English language dubbing. Fortunately, Criterion's white font subtitles, which so often are unreadable against pale backgrounds in black and white films, are saved by the widescreen black bars, which make for, at least, a readable contrast for the subtitles. As for features, there is an interview with film critic and historian Tony Rayns, on the film, and an interview of Imamura by Japanese film critic Tadao Sato. Imamura's interview, has a few good insights while Rayns' interview is also solid, with no great moments nor gaffes, although he makes a cogent observation on the essence of the film being comic; noting a late scene where a table collapses under Sadako's weight, after another harrowing experience with Hiraoko, as well as a scene with Masaru removing his grandfather's dentures at a ritual. There is also an insert booklet essay by James Quandt.

Intentions Of Murder is actually at its filmic best when not dealing with the ideas of rape and murder. Its symbolism is quite strong and well used, especially its animal metaphors, such as the equation of silkworms with the penis and used to show Sadako's odd feelings toward sex (note the smashed worm scene). Then there are Masaru's two mice, the smaller one of which kills and eats the larger one, fascinating the boy and encapsulating Sadako's ongoing battle with everything, as well as the treadmill they run on. Another great visual metaphor occurs when Sadako, several times, sees her reflection in the base of a hot iron, with each moment seeing her under a different sort of duress- be it physical or psychic. As a character portrait the film also succeeds, especially with its three main characters. Sadako is the most multi-faceted, but Hiraoko is not a caricature. His claims of love may seem contrived, but his evil, seen as a reaction to a death sentence, becomes believable, at least in Imamura's hands- see the scene after the first rape, where it's clear the man has a conscience, but also may simply be emotionally immature. Equally believable is Riichi's indifference, snobbery, and hypocrisy. The only throwaway character is the paper-thin Masuda, whose only payoff comes in the moment of her death. In many ways, the film is reminiscent of Roman Polanski's *Repulsion*, in that two young women, with obvious sexual abuse in their backgrounds, are left alone in a small home, only to have to fend off intruders and evil intentions. In Imamura's film Sadako rises above fear and insanity by actually engaging and fighting back, empowering herself, whereas the heroine of *Repulsion*, played by Catherine Deneuve, sinks into despair and insanity by doing nothing, and twice resorting to murder- an act Sadako cannot broach.

But, too often *Intentions Of Murder* goes on a few moments too long in a scene, as if Imamura is admiring the scene's cleverness, or really trying to hammer home a point. The worst example comes after Hiraoko's death. The film goes on nearly another twenty minutes when it could have been neatly summarized in two. Nonetheless, it's a good, occasionally very good film that, despite its flaws, is recommended viewing for its daring and successes. It is not a perfect film, but it is art, and fine art, at that.

DVD Review Of *Violence At Noon*
Copyright © by Dan Schneider, 2010

Nagisa Oshima's black and white 1966 *Violence At Noon* (*Hakuchu No Torima*) is the second film in The Criterion Collection's five DVD set called *Eclipse Series 21: Oshima's Outlaw Sixties*, and its an improvement over the first film, *Pleasures Of The Flesh*. That film had some great moments, but fell victim to Dumbest Possible Action tropes. This film has more excellent moments, more daring cinematography, a bit better acting and screenplay, and a more realistic basic psychology its characters follow. There are some moments that ring a bit false, and that is the reason the film gets pegged as a near-great film by me. But, strong arguments for greatness can be made. What was surprising, in looking up reviews for the film, both from its release and more recently, is how many critics complained that the film's non-linear time structure threw them. Given that we are over a decade and a half past Quentin Tarantino's *Pulp Fiction*, and given that film's far more schizoid time structure, one might forgive the older reviews, but the modern complaints border on the bizarre.

The film is a deconstruction of the pathologies that plague two couples who are part of a small mountain village that started a farming commune, and then suffered a flood, which wiped out much of their gains. The four major players are a suicide and his wife, Genji Hyuga (Rokko Toura) and Shino Shinozaki (Saeda Kawaguchi), a maid who fails in her attempt to suicide with him' and a serial rapist and killer known as the High Noon attacker, for the time of his crimes, and his schoolteacher wife, Eisuke Oyamada (Kei Sato) and Matsuko Koura (Akiko Koyama, the real life wife of Oshima). The film does follow a complex flashback structure, but some of the relationships can be divined early on, such as the guilt Matsuko feels over Genji's suicide. Early on we see her at his grave, and see him, as a ghost, whenever the camera shows her speaking to his memory. We know there is guilt, and it's only a matter of time that we learn its because she doubted his suicidal impulse. After he does so, after winning a record number of votes for the village assembly, he had asked Matsuko to marry him, then settled for Shino. Likewise, Shino was Eisuke's first choice, but he settled for Matsuko. The two women's bizarre love stories intertwine, and form the basis of the shell of protection they form for Eisuke, even though he has raped both women, Shino when she was unconscious after her failed suicide attempt, and under Genji's dangling corpse. Yet, Shino feels that, since he saved her before raping her, she somehow owes him protection, going so far as to even ask Matsuko's permission to offer her husband's name up as a suspect, in one of their written exchanges. Likewise, because of her masochistic love for him, Matsuko (who later suicides with Shino, who again survives) also protects her husband, despite his evident scorn for her. The film's ending, with Shino's lament that she's failed to die again and is only twenty, has a poignancy one might not expect from a film that spends most of its running time distanced from the four leads, peering into their lives with microscopic detachment.

Sato does a devastatingly convincing job as the serial killer (whom we learn has committed a total of 35 crimes), and nowhere is this better exemplified than in a late montage, where we learn that he has been arrested by the Tokyo police, and we see the two women running in an urban landscape as hear Eisuke's confession to the police. In it, he basically claims that had Shino given in to him, maybe things would have been different, only to hear a contradiction just seconds later, where he admits that even had he not met the two women in his life he'd have still been a rapscallion. This later montage is just one of many dazzling visuals in the film, and these set Oshima apart and above most filmmakers as a visual stylist. The use of black and white contrasts, the ambient use of noise contrasted to the staged village announcements on the P.A. system, the use of jump cuts and disorienting edits all absorb the viewer into the narrative. There are moments that other critics have pointed to as weak, specifically the women's actions to protect Eisuke, but looking back to that era, with what is known now of pathologies, the film actually is quite prescient over how the women in the killer's life react, and are manipulated by him, pressing their social values buttons all the way. And the device of pushing along the action via letters the two women exchange, while initially clunky, also has its roots in much of the correspondence between outliers of criminal activities, both in style and substance- the halting hesitancy of the missives and the reluctance to cooperate with Inspector Haraguchi (Fumio Watanabe) and the police. In effect, Oshima either knew what he was doing, or just got lucky in his interpretation of the criminal mind, for, certainly in Japanese cinema, the only better portrait of a sick mind I've seen is the kidnapper in Akira Kurosawa's *High And Low*. Furthermore, intended or not, the letters also take on a symbolic significance as the thin membrane that prevents Eisuke from capture. When an artist is able to benefit from even the unintended, then one knows that he has put into motion something of greatness and depth, for only those things can take on a life of their own.

But, most importantly is the foregrounding of the females' dilemmas over that of the psychopath, as it is perhaps the earliest film I've ever seen to deal with the subject of the enabling of bad behavior. The acting in this film is also a cut above that in *Pleasures Of The Flesh*. The four principals are all well cast and well acted. The screenplay, by Takeshi Tamura, from a culled from the headlines novel by Taijun Takeda, *Daylight Demon*, is well wrought and structured perfectly because a linear narrative would have revealed too much of the eventual plot via its moments of revelation. By scrambling things the viewer is left wondering whether or not the women's obsessions will cost them, or others, their lives. Played chronologically, Eisuke's capture would have been foretold, and inevitably so, due to the scenes given. The high contrast cinematography, by Akira Takada, is also first rate, especially in close-ups that exemplify the adage about the greatest landscape is the human mien. The film's score, by Hikaru Hayashi, is also excellent, perfectly blending elements that give an otherworldly feel to the film.

Like most Eclipse titles, there are only liner notes by film critic Michael Koresky as an extra, and the 99 minute long film is shown in a 2.35:1 aspect ratio. The transfer is quite crisp and clean. The subtitles, while often deadly in white, when on black and white films, actually work fairly well here, since the aspect ratio affords black bars on the top and bottom of the screen. The transfer of the film is good. Having seen these first two films, their power, and Oshima's growth, it makes me truly long to watch the third film in this boxed set, and that desire is something that no Hollywood film series has done in many years. Nagisa Oshima proved, with *Violence At Noon*, that he was a great director, even if one could nitpick this film's inclusion in that realm, and that's something most in the film business nowadays don't even strive for, so enjoy this film, and learn from it, because the monster that is presented in its is something most horror or thriller films cannot do, since the real monster is not the killer. You figure out the rest.

DVD Review of *Japanese Summer: Double Suicide*
Copyright © by Dan Schneider, 2010

The second film that Japanese film director Nagisa Oshima released, in 1967, was a black and white Absurdist film that plays out like a lost Oriental episode of *The Twilight Zone*, called *Japanese Summer: Double Suicide* (無理心中日本の夏 or *Muri Shinjū: Nihon No Natsu* or *Night of the Killer*). It is the least of the first four films I've seen in the five DVD set from The Criterion Collection, called *Eclipse Series 21: Oshima's Outlaw Sixties*, yet it still a good, and very interesting, film.

The film opens with a series of symbolic scenes of a horny, bizarrely coiffed 18 year old nymphomaniac, Nejiko (Keiko Sakurai), who cats around in search of, well....*dick*. She wants to get porked, stuffed, banged, slammed, balled, noodled, hammered, nailed, sliced, penetrated, aced, shafted, dicked, pricked, bowed, drilled in the worst way possible, and given her Dolly Parton sized rack, in a society known for flat-chested women, it would seem that she'll get her wish. The problem is that she exists in an Apocalyptic world, seemingly left over from a 1950s horror film, and the only guy she finds is a military recruit she somehow entices away from a parade over a deserted bridge in a large industrial city that seems otherwise unoccupied. His name is Otoko (Kei Sato), and he has a death wish, and, after a few symbolic scenes, the pair end up captured by a paramilitary gang that drags them off to a hideout, where they have tossed a number of other prisoners, as would be draftees into their battle. In scenes obviously patterned after Samuel Beckett (with a dose of Luigi Pirandello's Six Characters In Search Of An Author), the characters debate their fate, as well as how they will get back to whatever thing drives them. Along with the initial pair, there is an old man with a gun, a fat man who is tied up, because he is a killer with a knife, a seventeen year old boy (Masakazu Tamura) who desires to hold and shoot guns in gang warfare, and a few other lesser characters. Midway through the film, after several bouts of ego flagellation, the characters discover their captors have fled. Before they can formulate an exit strategy some of the gang members return, and state they were routed by their rivals, and that Tokyo is under siege by a white foreigner from America (an unbilled actor), who is a sniper clearly meant to represent both the Texas University sniper, Charles Whitman, and JFK assassin Lee Harvey Oswald (with references to Dallas), as he acts like the former, and is referenced as the latter.

They follow his plight via television, and the gangster that brings the tv acquires the nickname Toy, with his flunky called Television. After scenes of more conflict, resulting in the deaths of a number of the characters, the remaining characters- Toy, the teen boy, Nejiko, Otoko, and the old man, make it to the now seemingly war torn city, and drive past police barricades, which remain unseen, as if a sinister presence that hangs like a fug in mind, not body. They seemingly give themselves up to the foreigner, and say they are on his side. He speaks only English, and does not seem that bright. Despite his being less a human and more a force of nature, Nejiko offers her body to him, as she has all other males in the film. At first they break free of the police fire, and retreat among the ruins of the city. Then, one by one they die: the old man by police fire, the foreigner (shot by Toy), Toy- shot by the boy, who is shot by the police; leaving only the couple that opened the film, Nejiko and Otoko, who finally seems to be fulfilling Nejiko's fantasy of sex with him, as they prepare to die, fulfilling his wish of a suicide, now made double.

Like most Eclipse titles, there are only liner notes by film critic Michael Koresky as an extra, and the 99 minute long film is shown in a 2.35:1 aspect ratio. The transfer is quite crisp and clean. The subtitles, while often deadly in white, when on black and white films, actually work fairly well here, since the aspect ratio affords black bars on the top and bottom of the screen. The transfer of the film is good. The screenplay, by Oshima, Mamoru Sasaki, and Tsutomu Tamura, has moments, but is the major reasons the film often flails. At only 99 minutes, a good 15-20 minutes more of tightening would have helped, as for every two pointed scenes that is well acted there is one that is not. Hikaru Hayashi's musical score is first rate, and even the silences are placed well, as is the function of the television broadcast. Only the original *Night Of The Living Dead*, a film with many points in common with this one, despite differing genres, languages, and milieus, released a few months after this film, has ever used the device of a news broadcast as effectively. The cinematography by Yasuhiro Yoshioka is first rate, especially in a scene where the characters are debating life and death issues, and as each one speaks the camera whips to and from each speaker. Rare is that scene in film, but it immediately places one in the middle of the action.

  Most critics have copped out by stating the film is surreal (although it is not, for nothing supernatural occurs) or nihilistic (it is not, for the 'bad' people all eventually die in the film, do an ethical structure girds the film), when really it's pure Absurdism. Sometimes it aims for politics, other times for sexual interplay: note Nejiko's constant sexual mockery of the men she meets, none of whom seem willing to feed her the meat she craves. She is a ballbuster, but the best kind, one with no pretense of being anything else, although her belief that since the men won't screw her they are not real men, therefore they cannot be killers, is proven wrong. But, even though *Japanese Summer: Double Suicide* does not fully succeed in its aims, it does entertain, and it does provoke. Perhaps the ultimate proof that the film succeeds on some level is that its critiques on violence and thuggery were wholly missed by novelist and revolutionary Yukio Mishima, whose failed coup d'etat, just three years later, by his own band of private thugs, the Shield Society, played out in an eerily similar disastrous fashion to this film. When asked of his opinion on this film, Mishima is reported to have claimed he did not understand any of it. True or apocryphal, that claim sums up the going son within the film and without, for many. But it's that rare occasion when a full explanation is not needed, nor even wanted. *Oshima, hoi!*

DVD Review of *Sing A Song Of Sex*
Copyright © by Dan Schneider, 2010

  Nagisa Oshima's 1967 color film, *Sing A Song Of Sex* (*Nihon Shunka-Ko* or *A Treatise On Japanese Bawdy Songs*), is the third film in The Criterion Collection's 21st Eclipse package called Oshima's Outlaw Sixties, following *Pleasures Of The Flesh* and *Violence At Noon*, and of the three, it's the best, longest (103 minutes) and most daring. It's highly unusual to see any director create three consecutive films that consistently get better **and** more creatively daring. Along with these kudos is the fact that the film is also the most specifically 1960s in its feel, and by that I don't mean in the negative, in that it's dated poorly. Actually, it holds up well as a film that's merely set in that period, but could have been made in the last few years. The two prior films, while also excellent, were not nearly as grounded in the 60s zeitgeist. *Pleasures Of The Flesh* was a tale of criminality and irony, and could easily have been set any time in the last several centuries. So could *Violence At Noon*, set in a backwards Japanese village, and following the psychopathologies of two death-obsessed married couples. Not so with this film; it could only have been set in the Vietnam war era. And this fact also helps the film's dependence on symbolism, which is more present in this film than just about any other film I can think of, outside of Stanley Kubrick's *2001: A Space Odyssey*.
  The film's symbolism is rife through the film (see the early scenes of the black coated boys anomically walking across a snow covered sports field, that pulls back to reveal this seeming black and white loneliness reliefed against the color of Tokyo's urban mass), and penetrates as deeply as the very songs the four lead characters sing. It also starts early in the film, as it breaks from reality, when the leads start having delinquent fantasies that are furthered by a teacher that encourages their debauchery, then dies, possibly because of the actions (or inactions) of one of them, and the film ends becoming almost a treatise on the national destinies of Korea and Japan. But it opens with a focus on four high school seniors, who have just taken their entrance exams for college, the leader of the pack is the tallest, Nakamura (Ichiro Araki, a contemporary teen singing idol), Uede (Koji Iwabuchi), Hiroi (Kazuyoshi Kushida), and Maruyama (Hiroshi Sato). We first see them as bad boys who curse and smoke, and hit on girls. This set up owes an homage to the delinquent youth films that were rife in Japan, at the time, and which Oshima got his start in, but also with the zeitgeist of Nicholas ray's *Rebel Without A Cause*. They have a number of girls on their radar, but none more so than a Korean girl (Kazuko Tajima) whose name they do not know, but whom they dub 469, due to the number on her lecture hall seat. She dominates their thoughts and so does a mystery woman the quartet spies walking with their teacher, Mr. Otake (Juzo Itami). They hypothesize she is a prostitute, due to colored hair, but soon learn she was Otake's lover for the last seven years, named Takako Tanigawa (Akiko Koyama). The film makes no bones about its phallic influence.
  Later that night the boys end up partying with Otaka, and many other students- male and female. The teacher drunkenly discourses on the import of bawdy songs in Japanese history, and the girls coo over him. The song he teaches the boy, like *99 Barrels Of Beer On The Wall*, can be extended to infinity, and many reprises follow, but it begins:

> *Let's begin with the first case, hoi!*
> *Doing it with an only daughter, hoi, hoi!*
> *Ask her parents' permission first, hoi!*

Otake offers to put the four boys and three of the girls, up with him for a night at a hotel, which leads to the boys scheming to get laid as they play homo-erotic games in their underwater. After some failed comic attempts to woo the girls (see the rice cracker and donut scene), Nakamura goes to Otake's room, so get a pen, sees him passed out drunk, smells gas in the room, but does nothing to remedy the situation. In the morning the three girls are openly weeping, as Otake has died from gas poisoning, and the boys show little emotion. Then they try to startle the girls by claiming they had killed Otake.

As the girls take a train home, and the boys return to wander the city, they start singing one of the bawdy songs Otake extolled, and each fantasize about reaping 469 in the lecture hall. We see each of their fantasies, and each boy tries to outdo the next. Many critics point to this as the point in the film where the lines of reality blur with fantasy, but I think that line is crossed when Nakamura leaves Otake in his room, knowing there is gas. Since the rest of the film makes little logical sense after that, although much sense symbolically and metaphorically, and afterwards casts him as first among equals, it's likely that his guilt over leaving Otake alone triggers his fantasies of control, not only of the sexual destinies of assorted females in the film, but of his three buddies, whom he clearly sees as weak-willed without his guidance. After the shared rape fantasies Nakamura leaves his friends behind, and appears at the apartment of Takako, a woman who has sexually enticed him since he first saw her walking with Otake. Several scenes show him overpowering her, and possibly raping her, as he sings the bawdy song that acts as the four boys' rallying cry. Or, the scenes can be interpreted as a re-enactment of Nakamura's last moments with the passed out Otake. Yet, given that this could all be Nakamura's fantasy, and one he alone experiences, makes it all the more powerful when contrasted with the three other boys' experience of attending a university's Vietnam War protest, wherein Japanese hippies sing, in English, anti-war folks songs, such as *This Land Is Your Land*, *We Shall Overcome*, and *Michael Rowed The Boat Ashore*.

The juxtaposition of both competing scenes with each other- intimate luridity against mass harmony- makes for a truly surreal experience, and, knowing how overused and misused the term 'surreal' is I don't use it lightly. After these scenes play out, Takako and Nakamura go to the protest, and Nakamura is the first to announce his rape fantasy. The others follow suit, and 469 issues a challenge, as her speech on peace has been interrupted. She dares the boys to actually live out their fantasy in the lecture hall. So, all five of them, plus Takako and another female, head there. That all of this would go on in the presence of an adult, grieving for her lover, almost wholly suggests that this, too, is a fantasy- likely Nakamura's, and that it began with Otake's death. Why else would, when Nakamura's three pals, start undressing 469 in her seat, would Takako not scream bloody murder (or, for that mater, why wouldn't the anti-war protesters get the police to intervene in a bout of declared attempted rape)? All Takako does is discourse on the Japanese origin from Korea, which is a metaphorical parent-child one, to balance off the stated copulation of four Japanese males with a lone Korean female. After some give and take, Takako offers her body to the three hooligans to ravish, in place of 469. But, 469 declines the offer, and they carry her to the lecture hall front desk, but chicken out in raping her. That's when Nakamura strides forth, down to the desk, and strips 469 naked. She looks up at him and asks if this time it's for real. Nakamura assents, puts his hands about her neck to strangle her, and the film ends ambiguously, as in all dreams of a fantastical nature.

Yet, it's hard to think of a film so radical in its use of music, especially diegetically, when not a musical. It's as if the characters literally sing their own theme songs. The screenplay, by Oshima, Mamoru Sasaki, Toshio Tajima, and Tsutomu Tamura, is top notch, although traditional screenwriting would frown upon its disintegrative structure. But, as in *2001*, the end result is what matters, and the film deftly unnerves viewers even though little overt violence is shown. Part of this unnerving is due to the fantastic musical scoring of Hikaru Hayashi (as well as the deftly deployed silences), which disorients the from the visual images, although one suspects the impetus for the score was really

Oshima's, since all three films in the boxed set have great scores, and Hayashi did the last two. The cinematography, by Akira Takada, also is excellent, and he helmed all three films. It constantly makes usage of little subtleties to throw the viewer's mind out of synch with logic. In seeing these films, as well as those of the entire Japanese New Wave, it really shows up how dull and plain old lazy most contemporary filmmakers are. As with all Eclipse releases, there are no extra features, save for liner notes by film critic Michael Koresky, and only the white font subtitles Criterion usually offers. The film is shown, however, in a widescreen 2.35:1 aspect ratio, the original one released to theaters, and this affords the subtitles a good background to be seen against. The transfer of the film is good.

 Sing A Song Of Sex is a great film, whose meaning is as complex yet simple as *2001*'s, and may be the most important film on the youth counterculture of the Vietnam era that I've ever seen. It is not as technically good as Kubrick's *A Clockwork Orange*, which also features a gang of four rape-happy youngsters, but it's far more visceral and immediately condemning of its culture. It's also a film that, in light of the many ham-handed symbolic films in the four plus decades since, looks positively lean and brilliant in its startlingly simple conception and execution. And, it certainly has fantasy elements in common with Michelangelo Antonioni's two key counterculture films, *Blowup* (with its heroes' Mod looks and dress) and *Zabriskie Point* (with its hippy nihilism), while exploring identity and sexuality every bit as powerfully and radically as Ingmar Bergman's *Persona*, and pushing the boundaries of excessive length, in the drunken singing scenes with Otake, which are reminiscent of the drunken opening of John Cassavetes' *Faces*. But the film that it shares the deepest strains with is Lindsay Anderson's *If....*, another film on schoolboys predisposed to violence, which is daring in its construction, and ends with anarchic violence. Like that film, the viewer walks out wondering what really happened, yet satisfied with the dis-ease of wondering; and this is why *Sing A Song Of Sex* is the definitive counterculture film, for it recapitulates the essence of the 1960s, even as it embodies it. Nagisa Oshima, long may you sing.

Film Review Of *Kabei: Our Mother*
Copyright © by Dan Schneider, 2012

On February 5th, 1940, a college professor named Shigeru Nogami (Mitsugoro Bando) was rousted out of his peaceful family home by the Thought Police of Tokyo for having the subversive idea that the Sino-Japanese War (or, as Japan called it, *The China Incident*) was wrong, thus violating the idiotic Peace Preservation Law, and subjected to almost two years of imprisonment and torture until he died, not long after the Japanese bombing of Pearl Harbor. This incident, and its aftermath form the basis for the autobiographical 2007 film *Kabei: Our Mother* (母べえ), by director Yoji Yamada, based upon the memoir of Teruyo Nogami, the man's youngest daughter, and a longtime employee of Japanese filmmaker Akira Kurosawa.

The whole Nogami clan gives each other nicknames that end in -bei. Hence, Shigeru is Tobei; mother Kayo is Kabei, oldest daughter Hatsuko (Mirai Shida) is Hatsubei; and Teruyo (Miku Sato) is Terubei. During the two years of his arrest, Tobei's family is supported by a number of friends and relations; chief among them Tobei's former devoted pupil, Yamazaki 'Yama' Toru (Tadanobu Asano)- a klutzy, effete intellectual who is beloved by the girls and harbors a crush on Kabei; Tobei's sister Hisako (Rei Dan) - an art student who lusts for Yama, Uncle Senkichi (Tsurube Shofukutei)- a borderline pedophile and moocher, and others.

The 133 minute film, shot on elaborate sets, has an artificial feel to it that evokes something of Guy Maddin's works on Canada, and this is wielded to great effect, for there is a dreamy quality to the film that definitively tells even the casual viewer that they are watching a film, not a 'real thing.' Even before Tobei's abduction (and that's really what his Kafkan plight was) the family was poor, months behind on rent, and hounded by Kabei's classist and Militarist police chief father (Umenosuke Nakamura), who eventually disowns Kabei and the girls, when she refuses to divorce Tobei, because he cannot get over his loss of prestige for having a 'traitor' for a son-in-law. Many 'incidents' occur, which bonds the principals, but hope for Tobei's release is never really one of them. Yet, the film never devolves into *Terms Of Endearment* type of tearjerker, for this exploration of this clan's existence is, down to the minutia, utterly realistic. The characters may mouth nostra, on occasions, but it is rooted in their essence, as depicted by their total filmic presence. They are not caricatures nor stereotypes. Hell, they are not even archetypes, and yet we do *know* these people intimately, and personally, well before film's end. But this is evidence of the depth by which Yomada '*realizes*' them.

The ending of the film is a bit of a letdown, as the girls get a telegram where they find out Tobei dies in prison, Yama is drafted and dies at sea, Hisako dies of radiation poisoning, from the atom bomb, after leaving the family to attend to her own mother in Hiroshima, and even Kabei- who dies decades later (the 1980s or '90s, if fashions are an indicator) dies still wailing for her dead husband- the years have given her not an ounce of solace nor peace. This is NOT the stuff of tearjerkers, despite the claims of a number of superficial film critics. But the fact that the ending is an emotional downer is not why the ending fails; it is because the whole digression on actually showing Yama's boat being sunk, and him drowning, then having this related by a heretofore unknown character (Yama's best army buddy), is wholly inapt to the emotional and narrative tenor of the film, as it makes it seem as if Yama's feelings for Kabei are central to the narrative. They are not; they are mere shading, not essence. It should have been a brief voiceover. The death scene of Kabei, likewise, is not well done, and similarly could have been wrapped up with some narration. But, aside from the ending, the film succeeds admirably. Is it great cinema? No, for it breaks no new ground; it simply aims for the heart, and succeeds.

The screenplay is adapted from Teruyo Nogami's memoirs by Yamada and Emiko Hiramatsu, and it has a certain Yasujiro Ozu-like quality to it. In one scene, as example, Harubei complains of Uncle Senkichi's farting, after he makes inappropriate comments about her breasts. In another, she upbraids her father in a humorously punctilious manner for reading a newspaper and wearing a scarf as the family sups. The cinematography, by Mutsuo Naganuma is serviceable for, as the film is bound by set pieces, the camera is less an instrument of art than of eavesdropping. The film is subtitled in easy to read gold font, not dubbed, and shown streaming in a 16 x 9 widescreen. The film's score, by Isao Tomita, is classically based, as the music highlights scenes, but not necessarily their emotional content. In other words, the music does not direct emotions, it frames them.

The film does many things well, but nothing really great. As example, when the girls receive the telegram about their father's death, shortly thereafter, when Kabei and Yama go to retrieve the body for a funeral, a letter from Tobei arrives- his final letter, and Yamada wisely films the letter, showing how, even near death, the perverse Military government openly censors the man's words, as we see major portions blacked out. We get a sweet interlude at a beach, where Yama, who cannot swim, almost drowns after falling out of a rubber tire, and is saved by Kabei and two other men. In voiceover, Terubei informs the audience of the dark day that sealed Japan's doom: the bombing of Pearl Harbor, and correctly relates it as December 8th, which is what it was in Japan, for Japan is across the International Date Line. Furthermore, the radio broadcast spends more time on the Japanese attack on Singapore, which was, in Japanese circles, considered the far more important military victory.

All in all, *Kabei: Our Mother*, is a very good prose film- in the best sense, and one buoyed by much humor, even in the face of the blight of *de facto* national suicide- such as a scene at a neighborhood block association, where the members do not know whether to bow in the direction of the Imperial Palace, or the Emperor's vacation home, where he is currently staying, so they argue over which way to bow, then bow in all directions, out of exasperation, but it is not as good as Yamada's great *The Twilight Samurai*, which has some hints of the poetic, among other virtues. However, Yamada's film is a clinic in character development which, sans a poorly conceived ending, might have reached greater heights. As it is, though, it is worth watching, especially for an American audience, to get an idea of how the Japanese general populace suffered in the war *before* the atomic bombings. To know one's foe is to know, and to know is to appreciate.

Film Review Of *Revenge*
Copyright © by Dan Schneider, 2012

Watching the 1964 samurai film, *Revenge* (*Adauchi*), from director Tadashi Imai, is an interesting experience because, while the film is not na league with the best of that genre, from such masters as Masaki Kobayashi nor Akira Kurosawa, it is an excellent film: well acted, well written, with interesting to engaging cinematography and scoring. It just lacks….well, that oomph, that ineffable something that separates the merely good from the great. The story, essentially a fable, told in flashbacks, about the silliness of revenge, based in the samurai code of honor, is a good tack to take, for the samurai, in this film, are a far cry from the noble knights that inhabit the cosmos of Kurosawa's *Seven Samurai*, and the handling of this 'fall from grace,' is not as complex nor compelling as a similar theme that dominates Kobayashi's masterful *Samurai Rebellion*.

That being stated, and taken for what it is, *Revenge* is a hell of an entertaining, and quite well made, film with deeper implications than the surface level bares. Compared with the two other masterworks, however, its 'message,' that much of Japan's cultural history was laden with stupidity, violence, and oppression, is ladled on too thickly. To watch this film, one would scarcely consider that there were any positives to the Japanese system of yore, even as it lasted for over an eon. Imai's work is not as well known as many of his contemporaries, a dozen or more who- apart from the Holy Trinity of Kurosawa, Ozu, and Mizoguchi- have seen their excellent films and careers revived with the advents of, first, the DVD revolution, and now, instant streaming, as I saw this film on Netflix, and the basic reason for this, according to online biographies and critical claims, is because of the very factor that weighs this film down from potential greatness: the director's own tendency to hamhandedly beat his viewers over their heads with his political views; mostly Leftist and Marxist. Yes, we get it: the feudal system of Japan was corrupt, and the layety were bloodthirsty, ignorant savages who would have been well at home in the Roman Colosseum. Point made, and 10-4, Good Buddy. But, this threads its way through every moment of the film, which, while laden with a humor missing from other such films, never fully develops its characters, not lets us in to the 'real' reasons behind the family feud between the Ezaki and Okumo clans.

Yes, all parties are ignorant, macho, stupid, but there must be more, as the film's sober approach to many of the aspects, leading up to the end scene, never veers too deeply into satire, thereby negating the omnipresence of the near grotesques that litter the screen. Screenwriter Shinobi Hashimoto seems to be hamstrung, and there is almost a palpable tension between the way the characters are sometimes written and how the actors portray them, which leads me to believe the director tried to impose things into the script that were not there. Nonetheless, we see a bamboo fence being erected yo keep out the mob wanting to see a duel between the two samurai: Ezaki Shinpachi (Kin'nosuke Nakamura), a minor samurai who initiates the feud by responding to an off the cuff insult by a wealthier samurai, the oldest of the Okumo clan. Challenged to a duel by the wealthier samurai, Shinpachi wins, and also defeats the second oldest of the Okumo clan, when he schemes to waylay Shinpachi. Hence, while banished to a monastery run by a cynical monk, who gets off some of the funniest and best lines of the film, Shinpachi is still in danger. His older brother has cowardly agreed to let him have a public duel with the youngest of the Okumo brothers, knowing full well that they have schemed and rigged the system so that the youngest brother will be aided by six other samurai who will step in if Shinpachi does not willingly give up his life.

Knowing he is being set up, Shinpachi nonetheless agrees to the terms, even as his brother shows some decency, and offers to allow him to escape. But their mother wants

84

Shinpachi to restore family honor by allowing himself to be killed. Yet, the Okumos' plan is not the honorable death he has been told he will get. As he is led to the bamboo enclosed dueling area, the jeering mob curse and spit at him, then hurl objects, one of which draws blood. After some elaborate and meaningless ceremonies, the trap is sprung on Shinpachi, and instead of lying down to die, he springs up, and slowly starts killing off the six Okumo samurai. Then, the local village elders send in their own men to kill Shinpachi, whose label as a 'madman' is now shown to be false, for the treachery of the Okumos, in collusion with the local vassals of the Shogun, are clear. The film ends with Shinpachi being overwhelmed, and slowly bled to death. His brother then commits seppuku by his corpse, and the film ends with disgusted lower end swordsmen of the local lord drinking themselves to oblivion, disgusted by the turn of events they were forced to witness and participate in.

There is a brief attempt at a love story that, thankfully, goes nowhere, but even the ten or so minutes that it is shown onscreen is an utter waste and detraction from the 103 total minutes of the film. The film also posits that the corrupt system is wholly to blame, but it is the willfulness and stupidity, of both clans and their members, that leads to the unnecessary deaths of over a dozen people. The system is just the backdrop. Nakamura so dominates the film that all other characters become appendages. In a sense, it evokes Toshiro Mifune's best performances as a samurai, yet transcends them because Nakamura also shows vulnerability, fear, treachery. He is a man first, a samurai second.

I tried to watch the film on my television, but the 2.35:1 aspect ratio was cut off on the sides and the subtitles were cut off at the bottom. Watching it on a Kindle, turned sideways, made all the differences, and this film, made by the Toei Studio, and distributed by AnimEigo, has highly readable subtitles. Mostly in gold, but with green added for when two characters are in conversation, it almost makes subtitling fun to read. That stated, of course, a good dub job would have been far superior. The cinematography, by Shunichiro Nakao, is solid but not spectacular, and the same levels of competence attach to the work of editor Miyamoto Shintaro and the film's scoring, by Mayuzumi Toshiro. One area that should be noted, and that is the film's dialogue. While, overall, the film's screenplay is a mixed bag, screenwriter Shinobi Hashimoto does lace the film with conversations that seem 'realer' than in any other samurai film. The characters do not effect 'honor,' nor do they preen. Instead, they speak as if they were modern day longshoreman or steel workers. They speak of shit and stupidity to such a degree that the dialogue becomes realistic and timeless.

Overall, *Revenge* is not a timeless classic. It is, in a sense, too mired in its era of making, save for the dialogue, but it does have moments- quite a few, that are standout, and enough of these are so good that the film, overall, becomes a pleasure. Compared to the churn that is spat out of Hollywood, that's high praise, indeed.

Film Review of *The Twilight Samurai*
Copyright © by Dan Schneider, 2012

Yoji Yamada's 2002 film *The Twilight Samurai* (*Tasogare Seibei* or たそがれ清兵衛?) is a great film, but also a great samurai film, as it pushes the boundaries of what that subgenre of film can contain, much in the same way that Masaki Kobayashi's samurai films (*Harakiri* and *Samurai Rebellion*), in the 1960s, pushed the boundaries of that subgenre past the standards set by the great samurai films of Akira Kurosawa in the 1950s through early 1960s (*Seven Samurai*, *The Hidden Fortress*, *Throne Of Blood*). Whereas Kurosawa made classics of the genre, and Kobayashi added psychological heft to them, Yamada makes the samurai film realistic, for his titular samurai is not only an expert fighter, but a man plagued by doubts, failures, and diurnal do.

The Twilight Samurai runs 129 minutes in length, and details the simple pleasures and aspirations of a low level samurai in the waning days of that institution, a few years before the Meiji Restoration ended the rule of shoguns and restored the Emperor to the throne. That samurai is Seibei Iguchi (Hiroyuki Sanada), a widower, in debt over his wife's funeral costs, who works as a low level bureaucrat at a food storehouse, on a small salary, and takes care of his two daughters, Kayano (Miki Itô) and Ito (Erina Hashiguchi- the youngest daughter who narrates the tale from the future), and a senile mother (Reiko Kusamura). Because he does not go out and drink with his co-workers, after work, they mock him with the name *Tasogare Seibei* or *Twilight Seibei*. Because of his penury, he neglects his appearance, and even gets in trouble for being unbathed, when a visit from his clan's head embarrasses him.

When the sister, Tomoe (Rie Miyazawa), of his good friend Michinojo Iinuma (Mitsuru Fukikoshi), returns to their town, Seibei finds that old feelings and dreams of a life with her are aroused. She is newly divorced, after her brother petitioned for such when her husband turned out to be drunken and abusive. Slowly, Tomoe, Seibei, and his daughters, bond into a de facto family, but this is set asunder when Tomoe's ex, Koda, drunkenly comes to Iinuma's home and causes trouble. Seibei steps in, ends up defeating the drunk in a duel, even though he only has a stick, not a real sword. Iinuma asks his friend to marry his sister, but Seibei rejects the idea, claiming that Tomoe will only rue such a marriage, for she would have to accept a poorer lot in life with him, and his first wife never could. This temporarily ends the budding romance.

When an internal clan struggle causes strife, a rogue samurai, Zenemon Yogo (Min Tanaka), refuses to commit seppuku, and slays a samurai sent to kill him. Seibei is then anointed as the next choice to end the one man rebellion, for legend of his defeating Koda with a mere stick has grown. Even Zenemon had earlier come to see Seibei and request a duel, only to be turned down. Initially, Seibei refuses the 'honor' of killing the rebel samurai, but then the viewer sees how evil and corrupt the system is, as his higher ups subtly threaten and cajole him into going against his conscience. The next day, he confesses his feelings for Tomoe, but she has accepted an offer of marriage from someone else. Seibei says he's a fool, and goes off to face down Zenemon. Once at the samurai's home, they do not fight, but engage in a profound discussion of the state of life and samurais. Zenemon asks Seibei to let him run away, and they exchange tales of woe. Seibei sees much of his own struggles in Zenemon's tale, then errs in telling the other samurai that he has only a bamboo sword and a short sword. Whether or not the conversation was a diversion to feel Seibei out, or was genuine, is debatable. What is not debatable is that Zenemon immediately starts in with a duel after Seibei lets this information slip out. Despite being wounded, Seibei is victorious, and Zenemon dies. Seibei limps home, where his daughters and Tomoe greet him. Tomoe says she thought he would die, hugs him, and Ito tells the viewer that they were married, but their happiness lasted only three years, until her father was shot dead in the Meiji Restoration, and subsequent Boshin War. Ito refutes claims that her father was unlucky, and says that his life and loves were worthwhile.

While there are some nice shots of Japanese sites, by cinematographer Mutsuo Naganuma, *The Twilight Samurai* is a film driven by its screenplay and characters. Scripted by Yomada, Shuhei Fujisawa, and Yoshitaka Asama, the film plays out like an Oriental and historical John Cassavetes film, as it is loaded with realistic moments that stick in the viewer's mind. The film scoring, by Isao Tomita, is not noteworthy, save in not ever wrongly intruding on the emotions of the moment. The film swept awards at many festivals, and cleaned up at the 2003 Japanese Academy Awards, with 12 wins, and deserved all such plaudits, although it lost the Best Foreign Picture Oscar, that year, to the Canadian film, *The Barbarian Invasions*. The film was short in a fullscreen 1.33:1 aspect ratio, and the subtitles are in a white borderless font.

But, it is the numerous little moments that define this film's greatness, not extended battle scenes. Some that stick out are the bodies of dead peasants floating downstream; Seibei's laments that he would prefer to be a farmer than a samurai; his bolstering of Kayano's desire to 'book learn;' and many humorous asides- such as when one of Seibei's colleagues laments his poor eyesight, due to age, then states the teeth go first, then the eyes, and a colleague asks about number three (the phallus), and the old man says that went long ago. But the best scene occurs at film's end, in the conversation between Seibei and Zenemon, where, in *Apocalypse Now* fashion, Zenemon mocks Seibei as just an errand boy for the clan. Later, Zenemon takes his dead daughter's ashes, and scatters them violently. One truly believes that a scene like this happened, over and again, in real life, even though it is a first to be seen in such a film.

The Twilight Samurai has everything a great work of art should have- a great and affecting story, well developed and realistic characters, believable actions and in depth dialogue, a biting critique on life (the samurai seen as corporate middle managers, puppets of the upper classes), and all this with a modern pacing and scope. Yoji Yamada may not be as well known as many of the other Japanese directors of the 20th Century pantheon, but this film shows him capable of equaling their best. Maybe even bettering them.

Review Of *Ghidorah, The Three Headed Monster*
Copyright © by Dan Schneider, 2011

There is a moment toward the end of Ishiro Honda's 86 minute long, 1964 film, *Ghidorah, The Three Headed Monster* (aka *Three Giant Monsters: The Greatest Battle on Earth*, 三大怪獣 地球最大の決戦 or *San Daikaijū: Chikyū Saidai no Kessen*), that explains much as to why the Japanese kaiju film genre had such a great impact on young boys, worldwide, in the 1960s and 1970s. After the titular space monster has been on a rampage across the earth, terrestrial monsters Godzilla and Rodan (who have been fighting for some time) are approached by the caterpillar Mothra, who speaks to them in monster talk (translated by the Infant Island fairies to the Japanese characters) about teaming up with him to defend the earth. The fairies report that Mothra is not having any luck because Godzilla and Rodan just want to fight each other (to which one of the Japanese quips, 'What's wrong with these monsters, they're as stupid as humans!') because they don't care about what happens to the earth, nor to humans, who've never been good to them, and hate them. This sentiment- the monster as an outsider (or child as outsider to adults)- is one that resonates with young males intensely (as well as a humorous moment where the fairies quip on Godzilla's use of 'foul' language, pottymouthing, to Mothra- a reason why Godzilla is truly the King of the Monsters, and why so many young males found him, and that scene, so cool), and oddly always makes me tear up slightly, because I, as a youth, always got this point immediately, and identified with Godzilla, Rodan, and all the rest.

Even in this film, the monsters are only used by the humans, never treated as beings to marvel at nor respect. And, naturally, all three earth monsters team up and drive Ghidorah back to outer space (apparently little Mothra's silk, as he rides on Rodan, can overcome even Ghidorah), with Mothra and the fairies headed home, and waving goodbye to Godzilla and Rodan. So, even though this is not one of the better kaiju films, it's always had a special place in my heart, even as it is the film that marked Godzilla's Showa Era descent from invincible god-like force of nature to cartoonish over-sized superhero. As for the rest of the story, well, there's so little plot that it can be summed up this way: aside from the monster bash, a princess (Akiko Wakabayashi) from a Himalayan kingdom (whose casual dress resembles Elizabethan England's in frills and collars) has her plane blown up over the Sea Of Japan by assassins. She survived, and claims to be a Martian prophetess, warning of the confluence of monsters and the end of mankind. Assassins are dispatched to finish the job once the prophetess makes a media beachhead. A Tokyo detective (Yosuke Natsuki) tries to protect her, the fairies get involved, Ghidrah hatches from a meteorite egg, and, well, you know the rest.

The screenplay, by Shinichi Sekizawa, is serviceable, and Akira Ifukube's scoring is quite good. The best thing in the film though are Hajime Koizumi's well shot taiga forest scenes in the Japanese mountains, where Ghidrah's egg lands. Another point in the film's favor is the appearance of the great Takashi Shimura, as Dr. Tsukamoto, a psychiatrist who tries to get the princess to give up her claims of Martian heritage.

I watched the film on Netflix, and the presentation was from Clasic Media, but its picture quality was that of a VHS tape, not sharp as on a DVD remastered copy. And while *Ghidorah, The Three Headed Monster* is the listed title, the screen title is the American *Ghidrah, The Three Headed Monster* (Honda's first name is also listed as the Americanized *Inoshiro*). Either way, the film is not a classic kaiju offering, but one dear to my heart. Of course, there are some scenes I could do without, such as a reference to *Mothra Vs. Godzilla*, when one of the Japanese says that Mothra and Godzilla once fought, and Godzilla lost (as if!). There are also some silly scenes, such as Rodan and

Godzilla playing volleyball with a huge boulder, and typical examples of *Toho Science*- a term that refers to the film company's silly attempts at abusing science to make stupid things seem correct. In this film, two examples stick out. First is when Ghidorah's meteorite egg hits the taiga forest and there is no evidence of a crater, a forest fire, nor dead trees falling away from the impact and radiating outward. The second is when the princess's plane explodes and an 'expert' tells the detective that it's possible to survive an exploding plane because the explosion causes 'dimensional gaps to open up' and she must have fallen in one. Come again? Yet, she is rescued at sea (or so we are told).

Watching *Ghidorah, The Three Headed Monster* is like taking a time trip back to my earliest youth, where my friends and I would sneak into the old movie theaters to watch these films and be transported away from the gloom and grime, doom and crime, of inner city life. To see Godzilla and the others in nature, battling it, each other, and mankind, well, what more could a poor city kid ask for? Some times great film experiences can come from things other than great film art. Perhaps this is one of those moments. Perhaps not. But, for a brief time, I was young again, and the world was in the paws of creatures greater than man, and I was in full agreement with Godzilla and Rodan.

For a brief time.

www.ingramcontent.com/pod-product-compliance
Lightning Source LLC
Chambersburg PA
CBHW020602220526
45463CB00006B/2420